FINANCIAL MANAGEMENT
A PRACTICAL GUIDE TO VALUE CREATION

PATRICK C. GREGORY, MS, MBA, CRM, CWM, MFP

FIRST EDITION

UNIFIED BUSINESS TECHNOLOGIES PRESS
7 CANDLEWOOD DRIVE
AMHERST, NEW HAMPSHIRE 03031

Copyright © 2004 by Patrick C. Gregory

All rights reserved. No part of this publication may be reproduced or transmitted in any form or by any means, electronic or mechanical, including photocopy, recording, or any information storage and retrieval system, without permission in writing from the publisher.

This publication is designed to provide accurate and authoritative information on the subject matter. It is sold with the understanding that neither the author nor the publisher is engaged in rendering legal, investing, or any other professional service.

Published by

Requests for orders or permission to make copies should be directed to:

Peter Markwith
Unified Business Technologies Press
Voice: 603.930.4648 Fax: 603.672.3190
E-mail: PeterMarkwith@UnifiedBizTech.com

ISBN 0-9721489-6-5
Library of Congress Number 2004108027

July 2004

10 9 8 7 6 5 4 3 2 1

Printed in the United States

To my parents,
for their unyielding love and support.

PREFACE

Understanding financial management is critical in today's global marketplace. Unfortunately, most finance textbooks are either too simplistic or too advanced for business students and non-financial managers. *Financial Management: A Practical Guide to Value Creation* is designed to improve the reader's ability to make keen financial decisions that improve profitability while creating value for the owners of a company.

This book is designed for general managers, senior functional managers, and business students interested in the practice of financial management. It introduces innovative techniques in a practical, intuitive way, but assumes no prior knowledge beyond a rudimentary understanding of financial statements. Unlike most introductory texts, which are conceptual in nature, this book ties concepts to reality. In fact, the concepts covered in each chapter are applied to an actual company, which reinforces the reader's understanding of the subject matter. Practical examples are also integrated to demonstrate how the financial tools and techniques can be used to improve the decision making process.

Financial Management: A Practical Guide to Value Creation emphasizes the application and interpretation of analytical techniques used in decision-making. These innovative techniques have proved useful for putting financial problems into perspective and for helping managers anticipate the consequences of their actions. To the first time reader, these techniques may seem a bit overwhelming. However, you will see that the tools and techniques introduced throughout the text are all motivated by the goal of value creation.

Financial Management: A Practical Guide to Value Creation underscores the principles of financial management, which are applicable to all companies – both public and private. The text is organized into ten chapters: (1) Financial Management, (2) Financial Statements, (3) Financial Statement Analysis, (4) Financial Forecasting, (5) TVM: Lump Sum Cash Flows, (6) TVM: Multiple Cash Flows, (7) Capital Budgeting: Decision Rules, (8) Capital Budgeting: Cash Flow Projections, (9) Capital Budgeting: Cost of Capital, and (10) Risk and Return. The chapters follow a logical sequence built around the goal of value creation.

Managers must raise cash in order to finance investments that are expected to increase the firm's value. As a result, Part I begins with an articulation of the two basic questions that financial managers face: (1) What investments should the company make and (2) how should these capital expenditures be financed? In order to make sound investment decisions, the financial manager must be able to conduct a detailed financial analysis of the company. Through the analysis, the manager will develop an understanding of the company's past performance and the various forms of financing available for future endeavors. One of the first steps in conducting a detailed analysis is deconstructing the financial statements. As a result, Chapter 2 explains and illustrates how a company's financial statements are constructed, deconstructed, and interpreted. As an application, the financial statements of Urban Outfitters, Inc. are provided.

Part II reviews the techniques managers use to assess a company's current "financial health," plan its future development, and make decisions designed to improve its probability for success. Chapter 3 demonstrates the methods used to conduct a detailed financial analysis of a firm's liquidity position, operational efficiency, and management effectiveness. Chapter 4 explores financial planning and forecasting with particular emphasis on managing a company's growth potential. The financial analysis tools presented in these two chapters are applied to Urban Outfitters, using the statements presented in Chapter 2.

Time value of money is the process of calculating the value of an investment yesterday, today, and tomorrow. Time value concepts underlie virtually every topic in financial management, including capital budgeting and capital structure. In fact, a rudimentary understanding of these concepts is needed when evaluating different capital expenditures and determining the most appropriate financing source. For this reason, Chapters 5 and 6 in Part III are dedicated to time value of money.

Part IV demonstrates how managers make investment decisions (i.e., capital budgeting) that maximize the firm's value. Chapter 7 explores the net present value (NPV) rule and how to apply this technique to make value-enhancing investment decisions. A number of alternative approaches, including the internal rate of return (IRR), payback period, and profitability index are also explored. Chapter 8 illustrates how to estimate the cash flow generated by an investment proposal and assess the proposal's capacity to create value. Chapter 9 demonstrates the methods used to estimate the cost of capital, which is used as a hurdle rate in evaluating the cash flows generated by the investment.

The value added through effective investment and financing decisions will make the company more appealing to investors. Part V provides the measures of risk and return used by a company's various capital providers to evaluate firm performance.

FINANCIAL MANAGEMENT: CHAPTER SUMMARIES

Chapter 1   **Financial Management**   The goal of financial management is to create value for the owner(s) of the company through sound investment and financing decisions.

Chapter 2   **Financial Statements**   The balance sheet can be divided into two categories: real assets (that give the company is productive role) and financial assets (that are used to finance the acquisition of real assets). The income statement lists revenue, and ultimately net income, generated with the company's productive assets.

Chapter 3   **Financial Statement Analysis**   To make sound investment decisions, the financial manager must be able to conduct a detailed financial analysis of the company using the historical financial statements. Through the analysis, the manager will develop an understanding of the company's historical performance and the forms of financing available for investment.

Chapter 4   **Financial Forecasting**   The historical financial statements also provide the basis for projected – or pro forma – financial statements, which reflect the impact of the company's planned investments expenditures.

Chapter 5
Chapter 6   **Time Value of Money**   Time value of money is the process of calculating the value of an investment yesterday, today, and tomorrow. Time value concepts underlie virtually every topic in financial management. In fact, a rudimentary understanding of these concepts is needed when evaluating different corporate expenditures, determining the most appropriate financing source for the expenditures, and evaluating the effects of the expenditures on the company's present and future value.

Chapter 7
Chapter 8
Chapter 9   **Capital Budgeting**   The process of making investment decisions that maximize firm value is known as capital budgeting. The primary criterion used to evaluate proposed investments is net present value (NPV), which equates the present value of the investment's cash flows to its cost. NPV and other investment criteria are used to improve the decision making process.

Chapter 10   **Risk and Return**   The value added through effective investment and financing decisions will make the company more appealing to investors, and improve the company risk-return profile.

FINANCIAL MANAGEMENT: CHAPTER SEQUENCING

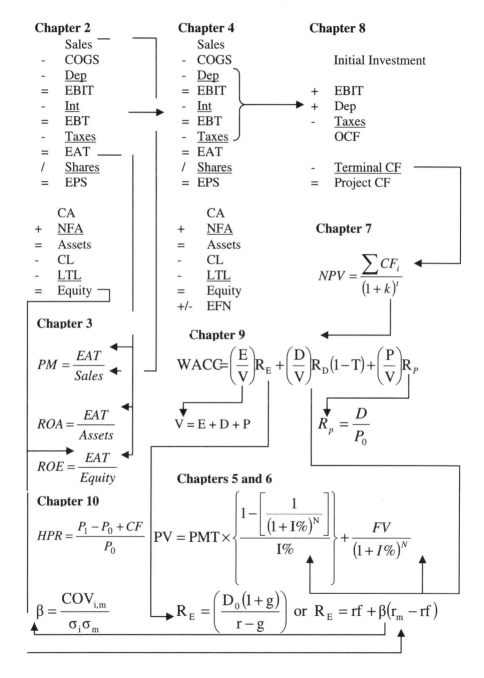

ABOUT THE AUTHOR

Patrick C. Gregory, MS, MBA, CRM, CWM, MFP

Patrick Gregory is a Professor of Finance at the McCallum Graduate School of Business at Bentley College, where he also serves as the Managing Director of the Hughey Center for Financial Services. An author, lecturer, and consultant, he was recently recognized as a "key professor" by *Business 2.0*. He is also the recipient of the Davis Fellowship and the 2003 Innovation in Teaching Award. Patrick is a frequent speaker on matters relating to investment, risk, and crisis management. He has provided commentary to *CNN, CNBC, NECN, WCVB-TV,* and *WBZ News*. He has also been cited in the *Wall Street Journal, Business Week, the Boston Globe, Boston Herald, Boston Business Journal, Los Angeles Times, Houston Chronicle, Computer World,* and *Yahoo! News*. Professor Gregory is the author of *Financial Management: A Practical Guide to Value Creation* and *Beating the Market*. His next book, *Thriving on Uncertainty: An Executive's Guide to Risk Management,* is expected to be published in January 2005.

As a founding member of Risk Alternatives, LLC, a Boston-based consulting practice, Patrick supervises the development of pragmatic solutions for corporations and financial institutions seeking to manage risk and create value in today's global marketplace. His clients include nonfinancial corporations, commercial, merchant and investment banks, energy companies, as well as insurance and reinsurance companies. Professor Gregory holds several professional designations. He is a Certified Risk Manager (CRM), Chartered Wealth Manager (CWM), and Master Financial Planner (MFP). He is also pursuing the Chartered Financial Analyst (CFA) and Financial Risk Manager (FRM) designations.

ACKNOWLEDGEMENTS

No literary work – fiction or nonfiction – can be attributed solely to the efforts of the author. This book is certainly no exception. Given the fact that the topics stem from a wide variety of theoretical and practical frameworks, I would first like to thank the many authors of text books and journal articles on financial management, which served as a foundation for this book.

Second, I would to thank Simin Kayhan, Manager of the Bentley College Trading Room, and David Milton, Assistant Professor of Finance at Bentley College, for their diligent work in ensuring the quality of the financial analysis conducted throughout the book. I am also obliged to my publisher, Unified Business Technologies Press, and to my staff, particularly Thanh Pham, Christopher Wong, and Michael Bartels.

Third, I would like to acknowledge the Hughey Center for Financial Services at Bentley College, which provided access to a full compliment of financial technologies. The practical examples that are integrated throughout the book would not have been possible without the data acquired from Reuters, Bloomberg, Factset Research Systems, and Decisioneering.

Last, but certainly not least, I would like to thank my family and friends for their patience, understanding, and invaluable support while I was writing this book.

PUBLISHER'S ACKNOWLEDGEMENTS

We are grateful to the following for permission to reproduce copyrighted materials:

- Figures 2.1, 2.5, and 2.7 were provided by MultexNet.

- Figure 2.2 was provided by Factset Research Systems.

- Figures A41.1, A81.3, and A82.3 were created using *Crystal Ball Pro®*.

- Figures 10.1, 10.2, and 10.3 are reproduced from *Stock, Bonds, Bills, and Inflation ® 2004 Yearbook*, Ibbotson and Associates.

- Figure A101.1 was created using data provided by Reuters.

In some instances, we have been unable to trace the owners of copyright material, and we would appreciate any information that would allow us to do so.

The concepts covered in each chapter are applied to actual companies in order to reinforce the reader's understanding of the subject matter. Practical examples are also integrated to demonstrate how the financial tools and techniques can be used to improve financial decision making. Company names, places, and incidents used in these examples are either the product of the author's imagination or are used fictitiously.

TABLE OF CONTENTS

PART I

CHAPTER 1 FINANCIAL MANAGEMENT — 27

1.1 What is Financial Management? — 27

1.2 The Financial Management Function — 28

1.3 Goal of Financial Management — 29

1.4 Business Models — 30

1.5 Legal Forms of Business Organization — 32

1.6 Organization of the Text — 37

CHAPTER 2 FINANCIAL STATEMENTS — 47

2.1 Income Statement — 48

2.2 Balance Sheet — 54

2.3 Cash Flow — 58

PART II

CHAPTER 3 FINANCIAL STATEMENT ANALYSIS — 65

3.1 Sources and Uses of Cash — 66

3.2 Cash Flow Analysis — 68

3.3 Common Size Statements (a.k.a. Vertical Analysis) — 75

3.4 Ratio Analysis	79

CHAPTER 4 FINANCIAL FORECASTING — 99

4.1 Financial Planning Process	100
4.2 Cash Budget	100
4.3 Growth Potential	104
4.4 Pro Forma Financial Statements	106

PART III

CHAPTER 5 TVM: LUMP SUM CASH FLOWS — 131

5.1 Future Value (FV)	132
5.2 Present Value (PV)	135
5.3 Discount Rate (I%)	137
5.4 Compounding Period (N)	138

CHAPTER 6 TVM: MULTIPLE CASH FLOWS — 145

6.1 Future Value of Multiple Cash Flows	145
6.2 Present Value of Multiple Cash Flows	148
6.3 Annuities	149
6.4 Amortization	153

PART IV

CHAPTER 7 CAPITAL BUDGETING: DECISION RULES   171

7.1 Net Present Value (NPV)   171

7.2 Internal Rate of Return   173

7.3 Payback Period   175

7.4 Profitability Index   176

CHAPTER 8 CAPITAL BUDGETING: CF PROJECTIONS   183

8.1 Cash Flow Patterns   184

8.2 Incremental Cash Flows   185

8.3 Project Cash Flows   186

8.4 Initial Investment   187

8.5 Operating Cash Flows   192

8.6 Terminal Cash Flow   194

8.7 Investment Criteria   196

8.8 Evaluating NPV Estimates   198

CHAPTER 9 CAPITAL BUDGETING: COST OF CAPITAL   221

9.1 Cost of Debt Capital   221

9.2 Cost of Equity Capital   226

9.3 Cost of Retained Earnings   229

9.4 Cost of New Issues of Common Equity — 230

9.5 Cost of Preferred Stock — 230

9.6 Weighted Average Cost of Capital — 231

9.7 Weighted Marginal Cost of Capital — 233

PART V

CHAPTER 10 RISK AND RETURN — **243**

10.1 Measures of Return — 244

10.2 Measures of Risk — 248

APPENDIX A MATHEMATICAL FORMULAS — **263**

APPENDIX B CALCULATOR KEYSTROKES — **271**

APPENDIX C FINANCIAL WEBSITES — **281**

APPENDIX D TVM TABLES — **285**

APPENDIX E FREQUENTLY USED SYMBOLS — **293**

APPENDIX F SOLUTIONS TO CHAPTER PROBLEMS — **295**

GLOSSARY — **299**

INDEX — **309**

List of Figures

Figure 1.1 The Finance Function	29
Figure 1.2 Legal Forms of Business Organization	34
Figure 2.1 Income Statement	49
Figure 2.2 Earnings per Share and Stock Prices	51
Figure 2.3 Corporate Tax Rate Schedule	53
Figure 2.4 Computed Tax	53
Figure 2.5 Balance Sheet	57
Figure 2.6 Components of the Statement of Cash Flows	58
Figure 2.7 Cash Flow Statement	59
Figure 3.1 Sources and Uses of Cash Statement	67
Figure 3.2 Common Size Balance Sheet	77
Figure 3.3 Common Size Income Statement	78
Figure 3.4 Industry Ratios	80
Figure 3.5 Time Trend Analysis	88
Figure 3.6 Peer Group Analysis	89
Figure 4.1 Short-term Planning Process	101
Figure 4.2 Cash Budget (Thousands $)	102
Figure 4.3 Cash Receipts (Thousands $)	103
Figure 4.4 Cash Disbursements	103
Figure 4.5 Pro Forma Income Statement	108
Figure 4.6 Pro Forma Balance Sheet	109
Figure A41.1 Sales Forecast	114
Figure A41.2 Historical Income Statement	116
Figure A41.3 Statistical Parameters	116
Figure A41.4 Assumption Cells	118
Figure A41.5 Forecast Statistics	119
Figure 5.1 Future Value	135
Figure 6.1 Future Value of Multiple Cash Flows (Example 1)	146
Figure 6.2 Future Value of Multiple Cash Flows (Example 2)	147

Figure 6.3 Present Value of Multiple Cash Flows	149
Figure 6.4 Amortization Schedule	155
Figure A61.1 Calculating Bond Values	156
Figure A61.2 Bond Values and Interest Rates	160
Figure 7.1 Project Rankings	177
Figure 8.1 Conventional Cash Flow Patterns	184
Figure 8.2 Nonconventional Cash Flow Patterns	185
Figure 8.3 MACRS Depreciation Classes	189
Figure 8.4 MACRS Depreciation Percentages	190
Figure 8.5 MACRS Depreciation Calculation	190
Figure 8.6 Pro Forma Income Statement	193
Figure 8.7 Operating Cash Flow	194
Figure 8.8 Cash Flow Components	195
Figure 8.9 Cash Flow Components (including Terminal Value)	196
Figure 8.10 Terminal Cash Flow	196
Figure 8.11 Scenario Analysis	199
Figure 8.12 Sensitivity Analysis	200
Figure 8.13 Mutually Exclusive Projects	200
Figure 8.14 Decision Tree	201
Figure A81.1 Assumption Cells	205
Figure A81.2 Forecast Cells	206
Figure A81.3 Crystal Ball Report	207
Figure A82.1 NPV Analysis	210
Figure A82.2 Budget-constrained Project Selection	212
Figure 9.1 Bond Ratings	225
Figure 9.2 Historical Dividends per Share	227
Figure 9.3 Weighted Marginal Cost of Capital	235
Figure 10.1 Total Returns	244
Figure 10.2 Wealth Indices of Investments	245
Figure 10.3 Total Income Returns and Capital Appreciation	246
Figure 10.4 Holding Period Returns	249

PART I

CHAPTER 1
FINANCIAL MANAGEMENT

Learning Objectives

After reading this chapter, you should be able to answer the following questions:

1. What is meant by financial management? What are the three categories of financial management decisions? What is the objective of financial management?
2. What are the primary activities of the financial manager, and how do these activities relate to the goal of financial management?
3. What are the basic forms of business organization? What are the advantages and disadvantages of each?

1.1 What is Financial Management?

Financial management involves the acquisition, financing, and management of firm assets for the purpose of creating value for the owner(s) of the company. In most business entities, the financial decisions can be broken into two broad categories: investing money, the so-called investment decision and raising money, often times referred to as the financing decision. The purpose of this text is to enable readers to make sound investing and financing decisions. These decisions are interrelated; the decision to invest in a new product or service will necessitate financing. Together, these decisions determine the value of a company. With a proper conceptual framework, joint decisions that maximize firm value can be reached.

The investment decision is the most important task in terms of value creation. The process of planning and managing a company's long-term investments is referred to as capital budgeting. Throughout the capital budgeting process, the financial manager strives to identify investment opportunities where the value generated by the investment (i.e., future cash flows) exceeds the cost of the investment. In fact, a key insight of modern finance is that value is created on the left-hand side of the balance sheet when companies make good investments – in, say, plant and equipment or R&D – which will ultimately increase the company's operating cash flows.

The second task, financing, dictates the makeup of the right-hand side of the balance sheet. In fact, capital structure refers to the specific mixture of debt (i.e., commercial loans and fixed income securities) and equity (i.e., retained earnings, common stock, and preferred stock) a company uses to finance its ongoing capital expenditures. The particular combination will vary by company and by industry. The objective of the financial manager is to find the combination of instruments providing the necessary funds at the lowest cost to the company.

1.2 The Financial Management Function

For large companies, the financial management functions fall under the purview of the company's chief financial officer (CFO), who oversees the activities of both the controller's and treasurer's office; see *Figure 1.1*. The controller manages the accounting and tax functions of the organization, while the treasurer directs the cash, credit, capital structure, and capital budgeting decisions. In smaller companies, these activities are often consolidated and handled by one individual. Regardless, the financial manager is obligated to make decisions that benefit the owner(s) of the company. To do so, he or she must relate each decision to its effect on the valuation of the company over time.

Figure 1.1 The Finance Function

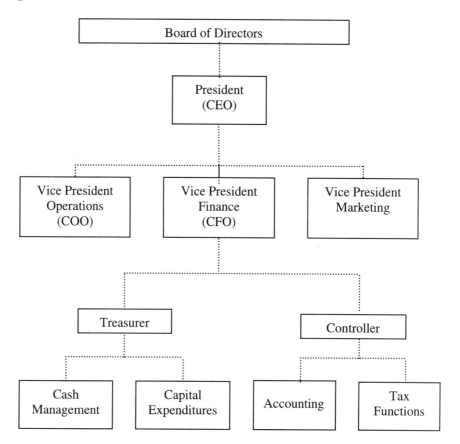

1.3 Goal of Financial Management

From the viewpoint of the owner(s), the goal of financial management is to maximize firm value. For a publicly traded corporation, maximizing firm value is equivalent to maximizing the current value of the common stock outstanding. Common stock represents ownership interest in the company, and as such, is equal to the value of owner's equity reported on the balance sheet. Thus, the goal of financial management for all companies – public or private – is to maximize the value of the company's owner's equity.

1.4 Business Models

Before you can begin analyzing the financial aspects of a company, you must understand its business model. Specifically, you should be able to identify (1) the nature of the business, (2) the industry and sector in which it operates, (3) its primary competitors, and (4) the company's sources of competitive advantage when compared to its competitors. With that, you can begin to articulate the company's business model.

This type of information is readily available for publicly-traded companies (i.e., those traded on an organized exchange). However, many of the companies are not publicly traded. In fact, many are not even corporations. As a result, it is useful to identify a publicly-traded "proxy company," which serves as a model for the company and provides a benchmark for performance as the company grows. For the purpose of this text, the proxy company will be Urban Outfitters, Inc. (ticker: URBN), a retail apparel company traded on Nasdaq.

Provided below is a brief description of Urban Outfitters and its business model.

Urban Outfitters, Inc. is a corporation headquartered in Philadelphia, Pennsylvania. The company, which was founded in 1970 by Chairman and President Richard Hayne, operates two segments: Urban Retail, which targets high school and college students between the ages of 15 and 25 and Anthropologie, targeting 30- to 45-year-old suburban women. Both segments offer lifestyle-oriented merchandise, fashion apparel, and accessories. In addition, each segment operates an e-commerce website.

Mr. Hayne opened the first store in Philadelphia near the University of Pennsylvania. Aimed at the student age group, the store sold used clothes, jeans, and ethnic apparel. A second store was opened in 1980 in Harvard Square in Cambridge, Massachusetts, and seven more opened near other college campuses during the 1980s. The company's wholesale business was established in 1984 and its first Anthopologie store opened in Wayne, Pennsylvania in 1992. A year later, in 1993, the company went public. At present, the company operates 60 Urban Outfitters stores and 50 Anthopologie stores in the United States, the District of Columbia, Canada, and the United Kingdom. Approximately 48 percent of the company's revenue is generated from Urban Outfitters, 44 percent from Anthropologie, and 12 percent through direct sales.

The companies primary competitors are Abercrombie & Fitch, Aeropostale, Chicos, dELiA*s, Hot Topic, and Pacific Sunwear. Under Mr. Hayne's watchful eye, senior management is targeting new locations in well established malls across the US. The company also plans to expand its presence in the UK, while boosting direct-to-consumer sales through catalogs distributed in the US, Canada, and the UK. As the company expands, it will continue to secure deep volume discounts from its vendors in order to reduce per-unit buying costs. To reduce handling and freight costs on its direct sales, the company also intends to establish a distribution center on the west coast. These measures are expected to generate revenue while reducing costs in order to enhance the company's bottom line.

We will follow Urban Outfitters throughout the text, examining how its experiences relate to the topics being addressed. In doing so, we will see that there are countless interactions among finance, marketing, and (operations) management. Moreover, the tools, techniques, and understanding that you will gain from this text will not only help you in your business career, but will also help you make educated personal investment decisions in the future.

1.5 Legal Forms of Business Organization

Aside from the company's business model, you should also understand the form of business organization chosen by the company. There are five primary forms of organization: sole proprietorship, partnership, corporation, S corporation, and limited liability company (LLC). The particular form of organization chosen will impact how profits and losses are distributed to the owners of the company, and how much each owner stands to lose if the company is not managed properly. Each form of business organization is outlined below.

Sole Proprietorship

A sole proprietorship is a business owned by one person. It is the simplest, least regulated, and most common form of organization in the United States. The owner keeps all the profits, but he or she has unlimited liability for business debts. What this means, ironically, is that the creditors of the business can file a claim against the personal assets of the owner to cover any unpaid liabilities. The life of a proprietorship is limited to the life of the owner, and the amount of equity that can be raised is limited to the proprietor's personal wealth. This limitation often means that the owner cannot take advantage of new business opportunities because of insufficient capital. Ownership may also be difficult to transfer since it requires the sale of the entire business to another party.

Partnerships: General and Limited

When two or more people engage in a business venture, a general or limited partnership can be formed. In a general partnership, all the partners share in the gains and losses of the company, and all have unlimited liability for partnership debts. The division of partnership gains and losses is specified in the partnership agreement, which can be an informal, oral agreement or a formal, written document. In a limited partnership, there are one or more limited partners who do not actively participate in the day-to-day activities of the business. As a result, the limited partner's liability for business debts is limited to the amount that he or she contributes. The benefits and drawbacks of a partnership are identical to those of a sole proprietorship. All partnership income flows through to the partners and is taxed at their marginal tax rate, and the amount of equity that can be raised is limited to the partners' combined contribution. Thus, a partnership's ability to grow can be seriously limited by an inability to raise sufficient capital to undertake value-enhancing investment opportunities. Ownership is not easily transferred because a new partnership must be formed. In addition, the partnership terminates when one of the general partners sells out or passes away. However, a limited partner's interest can be freely sold without the dissolution of the partnership.

Corporations

Large companies in the United States are almost always organized as corporations. For this reason, it is the dominant form of business organization in terms of sales in the US. A corporation is a legal entity separate and distinct from the owners of the company. As such, a corporation can enter contractual agreements to own property and borrow money. In addition, a corporation can serve as a partner in a partnership or own stock in a corporation or limited liability company. Starting a corporation is far more complicated than starting a sole proprietorship or partnership. It involves preparing a charter and a set of bylaws. The charter must contain the corporation's name, its business purpose, and the number of shares that can be issued.

Figure 1.2 Legal Forms of Business Organization

Type	Advantage	Disadvantage
Sole Proprietorship	1. Absolute control 2. Least regulated form of business 3. Owner keeps all the profits 4. All business income taxed as personal income 5. As simple to start as buying a business license and opening your doors	1. Unlimited liability for business debts 2. All business income is taxed as personal income 3. Life of the proprietorship is limited to owner's life 4. Amount of equity is limited to the proprietor's wealth 5. Ownership may be difficult to transfer
General Partnership	1. All partners share in losses, with general partners assuming larger amounts of liability 2. Partnership agreement can be as simple as an oral accord. 3. All business income taxed as personal income 4. Easy and inexpensive to form	1. All partners share in the company profits 2. All business income is taxed as personal income 3. Amount of equity is limited to the partners combined wealth 4. General partners have unlimited liability for partnership debts 5. The partnership terminates when one of the owners dies or sells 6. Ownership not easily transferred

Corporation	1. It is easy to transfer ownership 2. Limited liability for business debts 3. Much easier to raise equity capital 4. Treated as a separate legal entity 5. Most important form of business in terms of size and is recognized and understood by investors internationally	1. Starting a corporation is complicated 2. Requires the drafting of bylaws and the articles of incorporation to begin 3. Income is taxed twice 4. The process of corporate governance is complicated and inefficient 5. For legal purposes it must be the resident of a state and can be subject to state taxes
Limited Liability Company	1. One of the most versatile forms of business 2. The owners can be individuals, partnerships, trusts, corporations, or other LLC's 3. May be managed by its members or delegated to managers 4. Provides limited liability 5. Typically not subject to double taxation	1. Articles of organization must be drafted and filed under state law 2. If the LLC does not meet certain criteria, the IRS will consider it a corporation, subjecting it to double taxation 3. It is not a separate entity for tax purposes 4. It is typically required that a registration fee be paid per partner

The bylaws, on the other hand, are policies describing the corporation's day-to-day activities. For example, the bylaws describe how the members of the board of directors are selected. The owners – known as stockholders – do not manage the company's day-to-day activities. Instead, managers are appointed by the board of directors to administer the corporation's affair for the benefit of the stockholders.

One distinct advantage of the corporate form is that ownership can be readily transferred, and the life of the corporation is unlimited. The corporation also has the ability to borrow money so the stockholders' have limited liability. The most notable disadvantage is double taxation; that is, corporate profits are taxed twice – once at the corporate level when income is earned and again at the personal level when income is distributed to the stockholders.

S Corporation

An S corporation is a special type of corporation for federal income tax purposes. The corporation is formed in a manner similar to that of a regular corporation; however, it is treated like a partnership for income tax purposes. These corporations must satisfy the requirements of Subchapter S of the Internal Revenue code, which mandates that the corporation be domestic and have no more than 75 shareholders. In addition, nonresidents, C corporations, and partnerships are not eligible to own stock in the company.

Limited Liability Company

A limited liability company (LLC) is a relatively new form of business organization. It provides many of the same benefits of the S Corp without all the restrictions. An LLC is created under state law by filing articles of organization, which are similar to articles of incorporation filed by a corporation. The articles of organization set out the company's intended purpose, management structure, and number of shares to be issued. The owners, referred to as members, can be individuals, partnerships, trust, corporations or other LLCs. The company may be managed directly by its members or responsibility can be delegated to managers. An LLC provides the limited personal liability of a corporation and the flow-through taxation of partnerships and S corporations.

1.6 Organization of the Text

In this text, we will emphasize the maintenance and creation of wealth. Although this will involve attention to decision making techniques, the logic behind those techniques is stressed to ensure that you – the reader – do not lose sight of the concepts driving financial management and the creation of wealth.

This text is designed to explain what financial management is and to demonstrate how it can be used to create value. As noted in this chapter, financial managers face two broad questions: What investments should the company make and how should it pay for those investments?

In order to make sound investment decisions, the financial manager must be able to conduct a detailed financial analysis of the company. Through the analysis, the manager will develop an understanding of the company's past performance and the various forms of financing available for future endeavors. One of the first steps in conducting a detailed analysis is deconstructing the financial statements. As a result, Chapter 2 explains and illustrates how a company's financial statements – income statement, balance sheet, and cash flow statement – are constructed, deconstructed, and interpreted. As an application, the financial statements of Urban Outfitters, Inc. are provided.

Part II reviews the techniques managers use to assess a company's current "financial health," plan its future development, and make decisions designed to improve its probability for success. Chapter 3 demonstrates the methods used to conduct a detailed financial analysis of a firm's liquidity position, operational efficiency, and management effectiveness. Chapter 4 explores financial planning and forecasting with particular emphasis on managing a company's growth potential. The financial analysis tools presented in these two chapters are applied to Urban Outfitters, using the statements presented in Chapter 2.

Time value of money is the process of calculating the value of an investment yesterday, today, and tomorrow. Time value concepts underlie virtually every topic in financial management, including capital budgeting and capital structure. In fact, a rudimentary understanding of these concepts is needed when evaluating different corporate expenditures, determining the most appropriate financing source for the expenditures, and evaluating the effects of the expenditures on the company's present and future value. For this reason, Chapters 5 and 6 in Part III are dedicated to time value of money.

Part IV demonstrates how managers make investment decisions (i.e., capital budgeting) that maximize the firm's value. Chapter 7 explores the net present value (NPV) rule and how to apply this technique to make value-enhancing investment decisions. A number of alternative approaches, including the internal rate of return (IRR), payback period, and profitability index are also explored. Chapter 8 illustrates how to estimate the cash flow generated by an investment proposal and assess the proposal's capacity to create value. Chapter 9 demonstrates the methods used to estimate the cost of capital, which is used as a hurdle rate in evaluating the cash flows generated by the investment.

To create value, management must undertake capital expenditures that provide an adequate return on investment. The value added through effective investment and financing decisions will make the company more appealing to investors. Part V provides the measures of risk and return used by a company's various capital providers to evaluate firm performance.

Financial management is a quantitative discipline. To a first-time reader, the techniques outlined in the remaining chapters may seem a bit overwhelming. However, you will see that the tools and techniques introduced throughout this text are all motivated by our goal of value creation.

END OF CHAPTER PROBLEMS

Questions and Problems
Chapter 1

1. From a financial perspective, management should strive to:

    A. Maximize sales
    B. Maximize profits
    C. Avoid financial distress by limiting financial leverage
    D. Maintain stable earnings
    E. Maximize shareholder value

2. A company that is taxed like a partnership but provides its owners with limited liability is called a _____.

    A. Sole proprietorship
    B. General partnership
    C. Limited liability company
    D. Corporation
    E. None of the above

3. The process by which a firm decides which long-term investments to make is referred to as:

    A. Capital structure
    B. Capital budgeting
    C. Working capital management
    D. Financial accounting
    E. Managerial accounting

4. A properly articulated business model should include:

   A. Nature of the business
   B. Industry and sector in which the company operates
   C. Primary competitors
   D. Sources of competitive advantage
   E. All of the above

5. The amount of debt and equity that a company uses is referred to as:

   A. Financial management
   B. Capital budgeting
   C. Capital structure
   D. Investing activities
   E. None of the above

6. The form of business organization in which an individual owns all the company assets and is personally liable for all debts is known as:

   A. S corporation
   B. Limited liability company
   C. Sole proprietorship
   D. Limited partnership

7. Which of the following is not an advantage of a corporation?

   A. It is easy to transfer ownership
   B. Easier to raise equity capital
   C. Limited liability to the amount invested
   D. Easy and inexpensive to form
   E. Treated as a separate legal entity from those that invest in it

CHAPTER 1 Financial Management

8. The acquisition, financing, and management of firm assets for the purpose of creating value for the owner(s) of the company is referred to as:

    A. Working capital
    B. Capital budgeting
    C. Capital structure
    D. Financial management
    E. None of the above

9. Which form of business ownership will continue if there is the death of the owner(s)?

    A. Sole proprietorship
    B. Corporation
    C. Partnership
    D. All of the above
    E. None of the above

10. For a publicly traded company, maximizing current value per share is equivalent to:

    A. Maximizing sales
    B. Maximizing accounts receivable
    C. Maximizing shareholder wealth
    D. Maximizing working capital
    E. None of the above

CASE ANALYSIS

Company Analysis
Case 1.1

Using the resources at your disposal, write a detailed description for Pacific Sunwear (Ticker: PSUN), which is a retail apparel company operating in the Unites States. The description should include the following:

1. Form of business organization
2. Description of the company's business model
3. Overview of the company's organizational structure (board of directors, senior management, etc.)
4. Number of and location of stores
5. Number of employees
6. Market cap and number of shares outstanding
7. Recent performance (e.g., revenue, net income, price)
8. Exchange(s) on which the company's stock is traded
9. Any significant developments (mergers, acquisitions, strategic alliances, etc.) since its inception

This information is available in MultexNet. To access the data, follow the steps below.

1. Launch MultexNet
2. Type the ticker symbol in the dialog box
3. Click the radio button for "All Company Reports"
4. Click "Go"

The reports displayed on the screen should be downloaded using the "Download to Spreadsheet" button. Additional information can be acquired using the Hoover's Handbook in Bloomberg or various Internet sites. To access the data handbook, simply type in the ticker symbol, press the equity key, type HH and press Go (Type PSUN <Equity> HH).

If you do not have access to either MultexNet or Bloomberg, a number of Internet resources are available. Yahoo! Finance (http://finance.yahoo.com), for example, offers a company profile, significant events, key statistics, SEC filings, and competitor information. To access the information:

1. Launch Internet Explorer
2. Type finance.yahoo.com in the dialogue box and press enter
3. Type in the ticker symbol and press "Go"

The navigation bar on the left-hand side will line you to the desired data.

CASE ANALYSIS

Industry Analysis
Case 1.2

Using the information acquired for Case 1.1, complete a detailed analysis of Pacific Sunwear's industry. The analysis should include:

1. Description of the company's industry and sector
2. The size of the market ($ in annual sales) and the company's market share
3. A list of the company's primary competitors (by market cap, growth, performance, and valuation)
4. Description of the company's sources of competitive advantage

A list of the company's competitors can be obtained using Yahoo! Finance. To create a customized list, the screening tool in MultexNet must be used. The steps are provided below.

1. Launch MultexNet
2. Click the Screening Tool tab on the nav bar
3. In NetScreen Pro, click the "Add/Build" button. Under the Descriptive category, click "Industry Description" and click the "Select" button. The industry box will pop up. In the Industry box, check the radio button for the desired industry (e.g., retail apparel) and then click "Go." You will see the desired industry listed in the criterion box. Click "Go."
4. Click the hyperlink for the number of companies in the industry (e.g., 34). The report provides a list of companies in the industry. In the report, click the "Add/Remove/Arrange Columns" button. Under the Share Related Items Category, select "MktCap" and then click the ">" button to add market cap to your report.

5. In the report, click "Sort" and check the radio button to sort the data in descending order based on market cap. Click "Sort" to return to the report. The companies will now be listed in descending order of market cap (i.e., largest to smallest).

CHAPTER 2
FINANCIAL STATEMENTS

Learning Objectives

After reading this chapter, you should be able to answer the following questions:

1. What are the three financial statements included in a company's annual report?
2. What basic information is contained in the income statement and balance sheet?
3. What is the difference between ordinary income and capital gains? What is the difference between a company's average tax rate and its marginal tax rate?
4. How does the tax treatment of interest on company debt compare to the treatment of dividends paid to the company's owners?
5. What role does depreciation play in determining company cash flows? How can earnings after taxes, which is reported on the income statement, be adjusted to arrive at operating cash flow?
6. Describe the general format for the statement of cash flows. Describe the flow of funds through a company.

In order to make sound investment decisions, the financial manager must first conduct a detailed financial analysis of the company. Through the analysis, the manager will develop an understanding of the company's past performance and the various forms of financing available for future endeavors. One of the first steps in conducting a detailed analysis is deconstructing the financial statements. If the company is publicly held (i.e., traded on an established exchange such as NYSE or Nasdaq), the Securities and Exchange Commission (SEC) will require it to provide the financial statements and other relevant financial data to current and prospective investors by way of the annual report. Of the various company reports, the annual report is unquestionably the most important. Two types of information are provided through this report. First, there is a letter from the president or chairman of the board, which describes the company's performance over the past twelve months and discusses any new developments that will impact future operations. Next, the annual report presents the three financial statements – income statement, balance sheet, and statement of cash flows – along with any accompanying notes.

As noted in Chapter 1, the financial manager's primary goal is to create value. Value is a function of the cash flow generated through the company's capital expenditures (i.e., operations). How does the financial manager decide which expenditures are most likely to increase future earnings, and therefore, cash flows? How do investors and creditors determine the cost of capital provided to the company to finance these expenditures? The answer to both questions lies in a study of the financial statements. This chapter describes the basic financial statements, how they are used, and what type of information is needed by owners, investors, and creditors. Then, in Chapter 3, we will discuss how these statements can be manipulated to evaluate historical performance and to estimate cash flows, which will serve as a basis for making long-term investment decisions.

2.1 Income Statement

The income statement measures the performance of a company over time, usually on a quarterly or annual basis. The calculation of income is expressed in *Equation 2.1*.

Equation 2.1
Income (Loss) = Revenue – Expenses

Financial Management: A Practical Guide to Value Creation

The annual financial statements for our proxy company, Urban Outfitters, were downloaded using Multex.Net; see *Figure 2.1*. For a fee, MultexNet provides up to 20 years of historical financial statements. The most recent statements can also be obtained using the Annual Report Service, a free directly of online annual reports, or Yahoo Finance!.

To download financial statements for other companies, simply:
1. Launch MultexNet (double click the icon on the desktop)
2. Click the "Fundamentals" tab on the toolbar
3. Enter the ticker symbol for the company in the dialogue box
4. Click the radio button for "All Financial Reports"
5. Choose "Annual" from the drop down menu
6. Click "Go"

Figure 2.1 Income Statement

Urban Outfitters Inc. (Ticker: URBN)
Detailed Annual Income Statement
(Thousands of U.S. Dollars)

	12 Months Ending 01/31/03	12 Months Ending 01/31/02	12 Months Ending 01/31/01
Total Revenue	$ 422,754	$ 348,958	$ 295,333
Cost of Sales	$ 271,963	$ 235,311	$ 200,002
Selling/Gen./Admin.	$ 105,392	$ 88,149	$ 77,453
Total Expenses	$ 377,355	$ 323,460	$ 277,455
Interest, Net	$ 1,497	$ 318	$ 481
Other, Net	$ (823)	$ (594)	$ (572)
Income Before Taxes	$ 46,073	$ 25,222	$ 17,787
Income Taxes	$ 18,660	$ 10,215	$ 7,292
Income After Taxes	$ 27,413	$ 15,007	$ 10,495
EPS	$ 1.45	$ 0.87	$ 0.61

Calculating Net Income

For Urban Outfitters, the net income for fiscal year (FY) 2003 was $27,413,000. Revenue ($422,754,000) is calculated by multiplying units sold (Q) by unit price (S). Then, the company's various expenses ($395,341,000) are deducted to arrive at net income. Specifically, the cost of goods sold and deprecation are deducted from net sales to arrive at earnings before interest and taxes, or EBIT. The deduction for depreciation is an accounting entry. All assets are listed on the balance sheet in terms of book value; that is, historical cost less an adjustment for depreciation. Thus, depreciation represents an adjustment for the use of each asset each year. As a noncash expense, depreciation causes a difference between the company's income and cash flow.

In the process of determining taxable income (sometimes referred to as earnings before taxes or EBT), business entities are allowed to deduct operating expenses, as well as interest expense. The tax deductibility of these expenses reduces their actual (i.e., after tax) cost to the company. Interest income, on the other hand, is included as ordinary income and taxed at the company's applicable tax rate. The figure reported, $27,413,000, is net income (sometimes referred to as earnings after taxes) reported for FY 2003.

Equation 2.2

$$\text{Earnings Per Share (EPS)} = \frac{\text{Net Income}}{\text{Total Shares Outstanding}}$$

A company's net income (or loss) is often expressed on a per share basis and referred to – not surprisingly – as earnings per share (EPS). This figure is closely tracked by investors and other market professionals because it is positively correlated with the company's stock price; that is, an increase in earnings tends to increase the stock price of publicly traded companies, providing a return to the company's owners. *Figure*

2.2 illustrates the relationship between Urban Outfitter's earnings and stock price over a 12-month period.

Figure 2.2 Earnings per Share and Stock Prices

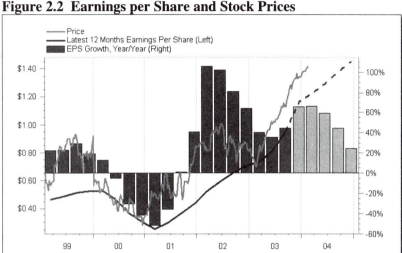

Source: FACTSET

Income generated by a company can be handled in one of two ways. It can either be paid out to the owner(s), typically in the form of dividends, or plowed back into the company as an addition to retained earnings. Dividends serve as a form of short-term return for the owners of a company. Unlike interest, dividends paid by a company are not a tax deductible expense. If the income generated for the current period is not paid out to the company's owner(s), it is plowed back into the company. These "additions to retained earnings" are used to finance future investments. If the investments are profitable, they will drive up future revenue and earnings; thereby providing a long-term return to the owner(s) of the company.

Accounting for Income

There are two methods that can be used to account for revenue and expenses. Cash basis accounting recognizes revenue when received and expenses when paid. With accrual basis accounting, on the other hand, revenue is recognized when earned and expenses when incurred. To understand the difference, consider a clothing manufacturer that sells a line of clothing on credit. If the manufacturer is a cash basis taxpayer, then the revenue would be realized when the money is ultimately collected. If the manufacturer has chosen the accrual basis, revenue would be recognized at the time of sale, regardless of when the cash is ultimately received. Thus, the accounting method – like depreciation – can lead to discrepancies between the income statement and statement of cash flows. Specifically, the income statement may not be representative of the flow of funds into and out of the company.

Tax Considerations

Taxes can be one of the largest cash outflows represented on the company's income statement. The tax rate used to calculate tax due is dependent on the form of business organization chosen. For instance, taxes on income generated by S Corps, LLCs, partnerships, and sole proprietorships are computed using the personal income tax schedules of the owner(s). The progressive tax rates for individuals are 15%, 28%, 31%, 36%, and 39.6%. Thus, as the taxpayer's taxable income rises, so too does the rate used to calculate the amount of tax due.

Similarly, corporations move through a progressive tax rate structure before settling on a constant rate. The corporate tax rate schedule for 2002 is presented in *Figure 2.3*. As the table illustrates, the first $50,000 of taxable income is taxed at a rate of 15%, the next $25,000 is taxed at 25%, and so on. For instance, assume that a company has $40 million in taxable income for the most recent fiscal year. What would be the amount of tax due? Applying the appropriate rates, the tax due would equal $14 million; see *Figure 2.4*.

Figure 2.3 Corporate Tax Rate Schedule

Taxable Income			Tax Rate
$0	-	$50,000	15%
50,001	-	75,000	25%
75,001	-	100,000	34%
100,001	-	335,000	39%
335,001	-	10,000,000	34%
10,000,001	-	15,000,000	35%

For planning purposes, it is often easier use the average or marginal tax rate. The average tax rate for a company can be computed by dividing total taxes paid by total taxable income. As such, the average rate is the percentage of income used to pay taxes. This is quite different from the marginal tax rate, which is the amount of tax payable on the next dollar of income earned. Not surprisingly, the marginal tax rate is used more frequently in constructing projected (i.e., pro forma) financial statements since any new cash flow will be taxed at that marginal rate. The marginal tax rate for Urban Outfitters would be 35%; the company's average tax rate would be 40.5% ($18,660,000 / $46,073,000).

Figure 2.4 Computed Tax

Taxable Income				Rate	Tax Due
$ -	-	$	50,000.00	15%	$ 7,500.00 [1]
$ 50,001.00	-	$	75,000.00	25%	$ 6,250.00 [2]
$ 75,001.00	-	$	100,000.00	34%	$ 8,500.00
$ 100,001.00	-	$	335,000.00	39%	$ 91,650.00
$ 335,001.00	-	$	10,000,000.00	34%	$ 3,286,100.00
$ 10,000,001.00	-	$	15,000,000.00	35%	$ 1,750,000.00
$ 15,000,001.00	-	$	18,333,333.00	38%	$ 1,266,666.54
$ 18,333,334+				35%	$ 7,583,333.45
					$14,000,000.00

Notes:
1. = ($50,000 x .15)
2. = ($75,000 - $50,000) x .25

Equation 2.3

$$\text{Average Tax Rate} = \frac{\text{Total Taxes Paid}}{\text{Taxable Income}}$$

2.2 Balance Sheet

While the income statement can be viewed as a video of the company's performance over a fixed period of time, the balance sheet can be seen as a still photograph of the firm on a particular day. That is why the income statement is dated "for the period ending 01/31/03" and the balance sheet is dated "as of 01/31/03." Is it surprising to you that Urban Outfitters' fiscal year ends on January 31 rather than December 31? It should not be. Most retail apparel companies have a fiscal year that ends in January so that the seasonal nature of the business can be accurately reflected. In general, retail apparel sales begin to increase in September with the holiday shopping season. Sales reach a peak in December, and then January reflects returns and other adjustments to sales experienced after the holidays.

The balance sheet is a convenient means of summarizing what a firm owns (i.e., assets), what a firm owes (i.e., liabilities), and the difference between the two (i.e., owner's equity); see *Figure 2.5*. A firm's real assets (i.e., assets listed on the left-hand side of the balance sheet) are those assets that provide the company with its productive capacity. Real assets include office equipment, machinery, and land. These assets are financed through either debt or equity, the so-called financial assets, which are listed on the right-hand side of the balance sheet. The use of debt – often times referred to as financial leverage - increases the company's ability to take on value-enhancing investments. However, it also increases the potential for financial distress and bankruptcy. Urban Outfitters, for instance, has a debt-to-equity ratio of 0.23 (0.19 / 0.81), which is less than the industry average of 0.36. If the ratio were to increase to, say, 0.39, the probability of bankruptcy would increase in turn. As a result, the cost of future capital would rise, reflecting the increased risk inherent in the company's operations.

Assets

There are two broad categories of (real) assets: current assets and long-term assets. Current assets are those assets that can be turned into cash relatively quickly. Cash, accounts receivable, and inventory are examples of current assets. Long-term assets, on the other hand, are used for more than one year. These assets can either be tangible, such as property, plant and equipment, or intangible, such as a trademarks and copyrights. The assets on the balance sheet are listed in terms of book value, which is the historical cost less applicable depreciation. As a result, the balance sheet may not reflect the true value of the firm. In fact, book value accounts for less than 20 percent of the market value of companies operating in today's service-based economy, where human capital and other "intangibles" account for a large proportion of a company's total value.

Assets are normally listed on the balance sheet in order of decreasing liquidity, meaning that the most liquid assets are listed first. A highly liquid asset is one that can be sold quickly without significant loss of value. One measure of liquidity that will be outlined in Chapter 3 is the current ratio, which is calculated by dividing current assets by current liabilities. The benchmark for the current ratio is 1.5. If the ratio is less than 1.5, the company does not have the current assets needed to meet those obligations coming due in the next twelve month. As a result, the company would either have to sell off productive assets to generate cash or raise funds externally through the issuance of debt or equity; both alternatives are costly.

In addition to cost, financial distress must also be considered. The more liquid assets a company holds, the less likely it is to experience financial distress. Unfortunately, liquid assets generally provide a lower rate of return, which brings us to an interesting question: What level of liquidity is acceptable? Let's consider an example. Urban Outfitter's current ratio is 3.36, indicating that the company has its current liabilities covered 3.36 times over. The ratio for the retail apparel industry is 2.4. Does this indicate that the company has too many liquid assets? Is the company operating inefficiently? Not necessarily. In this case, the additional liquid assets are needed to support the expansion efforts described in Chapter 1. If financed internally, the additional stores will provide a higher return on investment than if financed through the issuance of additional debt or equity, thereby creating value for the owner(s) of the company.

Liabilities & Owner's Equity

Liabilities are debts that a company is obligated to pay back. Like assets, liabilities can be delineated as either current or long-term. Current liabilities are due within one year; accounts payable is one example. Debts that are not due in the next 12 months are classified as long-term liabilities.

The difference between the value of the company's assets and liabilities is referred to as shareholder' equity. Equity is typically comprised of common and preferred stock, paid in capital, and retained earnings. This portion of the balance sheet is intended to reflect the fact that, if the firm were to sell off all its assets (i.e., liquidate) and use the money to pay off its debts, then whatever is left accrues to the owners of the company.

Figure 2.5 Balance Sheet

Urban Outfitters, Inc.
Detailed Annual Balance Sheet (Thousands $)

	As of 01/31/03	As of 01/31/02	As of 01/31/01
ASSETS			
Cash/Equivalents	$ 72,127	$ 28,251	$ 16,286
Investments	$ 7,379	$ 32	$ 314
Accounts Rcvbl.	$ 3,825	$ 4,691	$ 3,944
Doubtful Account	$ (563)	$ (562)	$ (500)
Inventories	$ 48,825	$ 41,086	$ 34,786
Prepaids	$ 8,633	$ 5,870	$ 7,302
Deferred Taxes	$ 4,358	$ 2,781	$ 2,841
Total Current	$ 144,584	$ 82,149	$ 64,973
Land	$ 543	$ 543	$ 543
Building	$ 4,331	$ 4,317	$ 3,383
Furnit./Fixtures	$ 44,487	$ 35,963	$ 32,527
Leasehold Imprv.	$ 121,878	$ 107,344	$ 89,120
Construction	$ 3,487	$ 7,280	$ 7,330
Prop. & Equip.	$ 10,056	$ 7,910	$ 7,484
Other Assets	$ 8,925	$ 7,448	$ 5,842
Depreciation	$ (75,935)	$ (57,852)	$ (42,486)
Investments	$ 15,640	$ -	$ -
Total Assets	$ 277,996	$ 195,102	$ 168,716
LIABILITIES & SHAREHOLDER EQUITY			
Accounts Payable	$ 19,186	$ 20,838	$ 19,387
Accrued Comp.	$ 5,197	$ 3,928	$ 1,775
Accrued Liabs.	$ 18,689	$ 16,064	$ 12,156
Total Current Liabs	$ 43,072	$ 40,830	$ 33,318
Long Term Debt	$ -	$ -	$ -
Deferred Rent	$ 10,539	$ 8,384	$ 5,786
Total Liabilities	$ 53,611	$ 49,214	$ 39,104
Common Stock	$ 2	$ 2	$ 2
Paid in Capital	$ 67,162	$ 17,872	$ 16,268
Retained Earns.	$ 157,221	$ 128,014	$ 113,342
Total Equity	$ 224,385	$ 145,888	$ 129,612

Equation 2.4
Assets = Liabilities + Shareholders' Equity

2.3 Cash Flow

As the name indicates, cash flow is the measure of the flow of funds (i.e., cash) into and out of the company over a historical period of time. The Statement of Cash Flows for Urban Outfitters is presented in *Figure 2.7*. The statement is divided into three broad sections: cash from operating activities ($41,791,000), cash from investing activities (-$45,602,000), and cash from financing activities ($47,402,000). A description of each component is provided in *Figure 2.6*.

Figure 2.6 Components of the Statement of Cash Flows

Cash from Operating Activities	The cash generated from the company's day-to-day activities (i.e., business operations).
Cash from Investing Activities	The cash used to invest in assets, as well as the proceeds from the sale of various assets, including property, plant, and equipment.
Cash from Financing Activities	The cash paid to investors or received from investors. For instance, any money received from the owner's of the company (i.e., equity) would be reflected here. Also included would be dividends paid to the owners.

Numerous methods used to evaluate the flow of funds – including free cash flow – will be explored in Chapters 3.

Figure 2.7 Cash Flow Statement

Urban Outfitters, Inc.
Detailed Annual Statement of Cash Flows (000's $)

	12 Months Ending 01/31/2003	12 Months Ending 01/31/2002	12 Months Ending 01/31/2001
OPERATING CASH FLOWS			
Net Income	$ 27,413	$ 15,007	$ 10,495
Depreciation	$ 18,208	$ 15,462	$ 11,997
Deferred Taxes	$ (3,079)	$ (1,274)	$ 199
Tax Benefit Options	$ 2,248	$ 323	$ -
Disposal of Assets	$ -	$ -	$ -
Prov. for Accts. Rcv.	$ 1	$ 62	$ (18)
Deferred Income	$ -	$ -	$ -
Receivables	$ 886	$ (753)	$ 1,399
Inventories	$ (7,554)	$ (6,348)	$ (7,918)
Prepaids	$ (2,718)	$ 1,120	$ 207
Payables/Accrued	$ 6,386	$ 9,141	$ 6,519
Cash From Operations	$ 41,791	$ 32,740	$ 22,880
INVESTING CASH FLOWS			
Capital Expenditures	$ (22,247)	$ (22,309)	$ (36,877)
Investments Purch.	$ -	$ -	$ -
Sale of Prop./Equip.	$ -	$ -	$ -
Purch. Invest. Sale	$ (43,585)	$ -	$ (600)
Sale of Investments	$ 20,230	$ 307	$ 19,930
Mat. of Investments	$ -	$ -	$ -
Cash From Investing	$ (45,602)	$ (22,002)	$ (17,547)
FINANCING CASH FLOWS			
Options/Warrants	$ 5,496	$ 1,281	$ -
Debt Issuance	$ -	$ -	$ -
Repayment of Debt	$ -	$ -	$ -
IPO Proceeds	$ -	$ -	$ -
Comm. Stk. Issuance	$ 41,546	$ -	$ -
Comm. Stk. Purchase	$ -	$ -	$ (1,412)
Cash From Financing	$ 47,042	$ 1,281	$ (1,412)
Foreign Exch Effects	$ 645	$ (54)	$ (362)
Net Change In Cash	$ 43,876	$ 11,965	$ 3,559

END OF CHAPTER PROBLEMS

Questions and Problems
Chapter 2

1. The amount of tax payable divided by the taxable income is referred to as:

    A. Average tax rate
    B. Marginal tax rate
    C. Taxable income
    D. Taxes paid

2. During 2000, Williams Global had sales of $2,000,000. Costs of goods sold, administrative and selling expenses, and depreciation expenses were $800,000, $300,000, and $500,000, respectively. In addition, the company had an interest expense of $150,000 and a tax rate of 35%. What was the company's net income?

    A. $87,500
    B. $162,500
    C. $227,500
    D. $422,500

3. Based on the information provided in Problem 2, what is the company's average tax rate?

    A. 20%
    B. 25%
    C. 30%
    D. 34%
    E. 35%

Financial Management: A Practical Guide to Value Creation   61

4. Barr Industries has 100,000 shares outstanding. EBIT is $1 million and interest paid is $200,000. If the corporate tax rate is 35%, what is Barr Industries' earnings per share?

   A. $3.72
   B. $4.40
   C. $5.20
   D. $5.28
   E. $8.00

5. What would be the corporate tax due on taxable income of $100,000?

   A. $22,250
   B. $25,000
   C. $27,500
   D. $30,000
   E. $34,000

6. Financial leverage _____ the firm's ability to take on value generating investments while _____ the probability of financial distress or bankruptcy.

   A. increases; decreasing
   B. increases; increasing
   C. does not affect; decreasing
   D. decreases; increasing
   E. decreases; decreasing

7. The amount of tax payable on the next dollar of income earned is the:

   A. Marginal tax rate
   B. Average tax rate
   C. Required tax rate
   D. Taxes due
   E. Total tax rate

8. The financial statement showing the snapshot of a company on a particular date is:

   A. Statement of cash flows
   B. Income statement
   C. Balance sheet
   D. Statement of retained earnings
   E. Tax reconciliation statement

9. Which of the following items is considered to be the most liquid?

   A. Inventory
   B. Patents
   C. Goodwill
   D. Long-term debt
   E. Fixed assets

10. Those assets that provide the company with its productive role are:

    A. Real assets
    B. Financial assets
    C. Productive assets
    D. Constructive assets

PART II

CHAPTER 3
FINANCIAL STATEMENT ANALYSIS

Learning Objectives

After reading this chapter, you should be able to answer the following questions.

1. What are the procedures used to construct a sources and uses of cash statement? How can it be used for financial decision-making?
2. Ratio analysis can be divided into five categories: payout, financial strength, profitability, management effectiveness, and efficiency ratios. What are the differences between each? How would the financial ratios be used by (1) management, (2) current or prospective investors, and (3) creditors?
3. What is liquidity? Which ratio(s) can be used to assess a company's liquidity position?
4. What is leverage? Which ratio(s) can be used to assess a company's degree of financial leverage? Which ratio(s) can be used to assess the company's ability to meet the interest payments associated with the outstanding liabilities?
5. What is difference between profit margin, return on assets, and return on equity? Which ratio is scrutinized by the owners of the company? Why?
6. What is the difference between time trend and peer group analysis?
7. What are common size statements? How would a common size income statement be constructed? Which ratio of profitability can be found on a common size income statement? How would a common size balance sheet be constructed?

Financial statement analysis is important to a wide range of individuals, including investors, creditors, and regulators. It is used to diagnose the current "financial health" of the company and to evaluate the financial consequences of management's ongoing decisions.

Based on the information presented in Chapter 2, it should be evident that the financial statements do not reflect economic reality. While the objective of accounting is to report financial information in a form that is useful for decision making purposes, the information often times does not come in that form. So, the financial manager must restructure the information to make it useful. Financial statement analysis includes the development of (1) a sources and uses of cash statement, (2) common size statements, and (3) financial ratios. Each form of analysis is addressed in detail below.

3.1 Sources and Uses of Cash

Whenever possible, it is advantageous for a company to finance its investments through internal funds (i.e., cash). For this reason, the first step in conducting a detailed financial analysis is to track the flow of cash into and out of the company through a Sources and Uses of Cash Statement. Activities that bring cash into the company are referred to as a source of cash. By contrast, those activities that involve spending cash are known as a use of cash. Constructing the statement is a three-step process:

1. Obtain at least two years of balance sheet data.
2. Calculate the change in each account value over the time period in question.
3. Determine if the change represents a source or use of cash as follows: An increase in an asset account (i.e., the left side) or a

Figure 3.1 Sources and Uses of Cash Statement
Urban Outfitters, Inc.
Sources and Uses of Cash Statement (Thousands $)

	As of 01/31/03	As of 01/31/02	Change	Source or Use?
ASSETS				
Cash/Equivalents	$ 72,127	$ 28,251	$ 43,876	
Investments	$ 7,379	$ 32	$ 7,347	Use
Accounts Rcvbl.	$ 3,825	$ 4,691	$ (866)	Source
Doubtful Account	$ (563)	$ (562)	$ (1)	Source
Inventories	$ 48,825	$ 41,086	$ 7,739	Use
Prepaids	$ 8,633	$ 5,870	$ 2,763	Use
Deferred Taxes	$ 4,358	$ 2,781	$ 1,577	Use
Total Current Assets	$ 144,584	$ 82,149	$ 62,435	Use
Land	$ 543	$ 543	$ -	Use
Building	$ 4,331	$ 4,317	$ 14	Use
Furnit./Fixtures	$ 44,487	$ 35,963	$ 8,524	Use
Leasehold Imprv.	$ 121,878	$ 107,344	$ 14,534	Use
Construction	$ 3,487	$ 7,280	$ (3,793)	Source
Prop. & Equip.	$ 10,056	$ 7,910	$ 2,146	Use
Other Assets	$ 8,925	$ 7,448	$ 1,477	Use
Depreciation	$ (75,935)	$ 57,852)	$ (18,083)	Source
Investments	$ 15,640	$ -	$ 15,640	Use
Total Assets	$ 277,996	$ 195,102	$ 82,894	Use
LIABILITIES & SHAREHOLDER EQUITY				
Accounts Payable	$ 19,186	$ 20,838	$ (1,652)	Use
Accrued Comp.	$ 5,197	$ 3,928	$ 1,269	Source
Accrued Liabs.	$ 18,689	$ 16,064	$ 2,625	Source
Total Current Liabs	$ 43,072	$ 40,830	$ 2,242	Source
Deferred Rent	$ 10,539	$ 8,384	$ 2,155	Source
Total Liabilities	$ 53,611	$ 49,214	$ 4,397	Source
Common Stock	$ 2	$ 2	$ -	Use
Paid in Capital	$ 67,162	$ 17,872	$ 49,290	Source
Retained Earns.	$ 157,221	$ 128,014	$ 29,207	Source
Total Equity	$ 224,385	$ 145,888	$ 78,497	Source

decrease in a liability account (i.e., the right side) represents a use of cash; likewise, a decrease in an asset account or an increase in a liability account constitutes a source of cash.

A Sources and Uses of Cash Statement for Urban Outfitters is provided in *Figure 3.1*. Note that the statement was created using the balance sheet for FY 2002 and 2003. Consider an asset account such as inventory, which grew from $41,086,000 in 2002 to $48,825,000 in 2003. Does the change represent a source or use of cash? It is a use of cash because the asset account increased. In other words, the company used cash to acquire additional inventory. Accounts payable decreased from 20,838,000 to 19,186,000. Would this be considered a source or use of cash? Again, it is a use of cash because there was a decrease in a liability account. Thus, the company used cash to pay off outstanding debts.

To understand the change in retained earnings, we must refer to the income statement. As you can see, the $27,413,000 increase in retained earnings can be calculated by taking the difference between the 2002 and 2003 figures ($156,529,000 - $129,116,000). This is the same figure reported as net income for 2003. Thus, the company retained all of the income earned in 2003; nothing was paid to the owners in the form of dividends. Thus, the increase in retained earnings would be considered a source of cash.

3.2 Cash Flow Analysis

Cash Flow from Assets

A measure of cash flow commonly used in investment selection (i.e., capital budgeting) is cash flow from assets, which can be calculated using information from the financial statements. At a basic level, cash flow from assets is comprised of three components: operating cash flow, capital spending, and changes in net working capital. Operating cash flow is the cash flow generated through the company's day-to-day activities; funds associated with the company's financing activities (e.g., interest costs) are not included in the calculation since they do not represent an operating expense. Operating cash flow is an important number because it tells us, at a basic level, whether or not the inflows from the company's operations are sufficient to cover its everyday cash outflows. For this reason, a negative operating cash flow is often a sign of trouble. To calculate operating cash flow, all costs – except depreciation and financing expenses – are deducted from revenue.

Equation 3.1
Operating Cash Flow = EBIT + Depreciation – Taxes

For Urban Outfitters, the operating cash flow would be $45,621,000 ($46,073,000 + $18,208,000 - $18,660,000).

Capital spending refers to the net spending on fixed assets (i.e., purchase of fixed assets less the sale of fixed assets plus any applicable depreciation) over the past twelve months. Just as with operating cash flow, depreciation must be added back since it represents a noncash expense. Could net capital spending be negative? Yes, if the firm sold off more assets than it purchased. In the case of Urban Outfitters, the capital spending during 2003 was positive ($40,085,000).

Equation 3.2
Capital Spending = Ending Net Fixed Assets – Beginning Net Fixed
                Assets + Depreciation
                = $184,782,000 - $163,357,000 + $18,660,000
                = $40,085,000

Changes in net working capital, not surprisingly, is a measure of the change in working capital over the period in question. Working capital refers to a firm's short-term assets, such as cash, accounts receivable, and inventory, and its short-term liabilities, such as money owed to the government (e.g., taxes payable) and business partners (e.g., accounts payable). Managing working capital ensures that the company will have sufficient resources to undertake new investment opportunities through the use of internal funds.

The difference between beginning and ending net working capital represents the change in net working capital for the period. For Urban Outfitters, it would be $101,512,000 ($144,584,000 - $43,072,000) in ending networking capital less $41,319,000 ($82,149,000 - $40,830,000) in beginning net working capital, or $60,193.

Equation 3.3
Change in Net Working Capital = Ending NWC – Beginning NWC

With the three components defined, cash flow from assets can be determined by subtracting the investment in fixed assets and any change in net working capital from operating cash flows. The cash flow from assets for Urban Outfitters is -$54,657,000. Is the negative cash flow problematic? No, not necessarily. It is not unusual for a growing company to have a negative cash flow. A negative cash flow means that the firm raised more money by issuing debt and selling stock than it paid out to owners and creditors that year.

Equation 3.4
Cash Flow = Operating Cash Flow – Capital Spending – Changes in Net Working Capital
= $45,621,000 -$40,085,000 - $60,193,000
= -$54,657,000

Free Cash Flow

Another popular cash flow model – free cash flow – can be used to value an entire company or particular divisions within a company. Free cash flow (FCF) is the cash available for distribution to owner(s) after the company has made the investment in fixed assets and working capital necessary to support operations. Because FCF represents the cash available for distribution, it can be used by the financial manager as a means of making the company more attractive to potential investors.

The principal source of capital for any company is investors; that is shareholders and creditors. Investors are compensated for the capital they provide; payment is provided in the form of interest on debt and dividends and capital appreciation on equity. Capital can also be acquired through short-term loans from the company's employees, suppliers, and tax authorities in the form of accrued wages, accounts payable, and accrued taxes.

For the purpose of calculating FCF, a company's assets must be divided into two categories: operating assets such as cash, accounts receivable, inventories, and fixed assets used to support the company's operations, and non-operating assets, which include investments, property being held for a future use, and so on. If the financial manager can generate significant cash flow with a relatively small investment in operating assets, it will reduce the amount of capital needed, thereby increasing the return on investment.

The current assets a company uses in operations – cash, accounts receivable, and inventory – are called operating working capital. The current liabilities – particularly accounts payable and accruals – that arise through the company's operations reduce the amount of capital that must be raised from investors. By deducting these current liabilities from operating working capital, we can arrive at net operating working capital.

Using the financial statement data for Urban Outfitters, the net operating working capital can be determined. In 2003, the company had $81,705,000 in net operating working capital.

Equation 3.5
Net Operating Working Capital $_{2003}$ = (Cash + AR + INV)$_{2003}$ − (AP + Accruals)$_{2003}$

$$= \$124{,}777{,}000 - \$43{,}072{,}000$$
$$= \$81{,}705{,}000$$

Equation 3.6
Total Operating Capital $_{2003}$ = Net Operating Working Capital$_{2003}$ + Net Fixed Assets$_{2003}$

$$= \$81{,}705{,}000 + \$108{,}850{,}000$$
$$= \$190{,}555{,}000$$

By combining a company's net operating capital with its net investment in fixed asset, the total fixed assets for the period can be determined. In the case of Urban Outfitters, total operating capital increased from $138,708,000 in 2002 to $190,555,000 in 2003.

Net Operating Working Capital $_{2002}$ = (Cash + AR + INV) $_{2002}$ − (AP + Accruals) $_{2003}$

$$= \$74{,}028{,}000 - \$40{,}830{,}000$$
$$= \$33{,}198{,}000$$

Total Operating Capital $_{2002}$ = Net Operating Working Capital + Net Fixed Assets

$$= \$33{,}198{,}000 + \$105{,}510{,}000$$
$$= \$138{,}708{,}000$$

The increase in total operating capital from one year to the next is known as the net investment in operating capital. Urban Outfitters made a net investment in operating capital of $51,847,000 ($190,555,000 - $138,708,000).

Equation 3.9
Net Investment in Operating Capital = $190,555,000 - $138,708,000
= $51,847,000

To determine the gross investment in operating capital, all non-cash expenses must be taken into consideration. Since Urban Outfitters reported $18,208,000 in depreciation in 2003, the company's gross investment in operating capital was $70,055,000.

Equation 3.10
Gross Investment in Operating Capital = Net Investment + Depreciation
= $51,847,000 + $18,208,000
= $70,055,000

Two companies with differing debt structures can have identical operating performance but report significantly different income in any given year. Specifically, the company with more debt will report lower income as a result of interest costs. For this reason, net income does not always provide an accurate measure of a company's operating performance. A more appropriate gauge is known as net operating profit after taxes (NOPAT), which is the amount of income a company would generate if it had no debt.

Using data from the income statement, Urban Outfitters 2003 NOPAT was $27,413,435.

Equation 3.7
NOPAT = EBIT x (1 − Tax Rate)
    = $46,073,000 x (1 − 40.50%)
    = $27,413,435

This figure would be compared to the NOPAT for competitors like Abercrombie & Fitch, Hot Topic, and Pacific Sunwear when evaluating the company's performance over the past twelve months. It could also be used as a substitute for net income when calculating financial ratios such as profit margin, return on assets, and return on equity, which are described in the next section.

For Urban Outfitters, where depreciation is the only non-cash expense, the 2003 operating cash flow was:

Equation 3.8
OCF = NOPAT + Depreciation
    = $27,413,435 + $18,208,000
    = $45,621,435

Note: Equation 3.8 can also be stated as EBIT − Taxes + Depreciation as noted above.

With this information, the free cash flow for 2003 can be calculated. In the case of Urban Outfitter's, free cash flow was -$24,433,565.

Equation 3.11
Free Cash Flow = Operating Cash Flow − Gross Investment in Operating Capital
    = $45,621,435 - $70,055,000
    = -$24,433,565

An algebraically equivalent equation is:

Equation 3.12
Free Cash Flow = NOPAT − Net Investment in Operating Capital
             = $27,413,435 - $51,847,000
             = -$24,433,565

In the above example, Urban Outfitter's free cash flow is negative. Free cash flow represents the amount of cash available for distribution to investors. Generally, when free cash flow is negative, an analyst or investor would need to examine the company's growth prospects and management's operational acumen to determine if NOPAT is negative and the likelihood that the trend will continue. In this case, Urban Outfitter's NOPAT was positive, and the negative free cash flow was the result of the company's investments in operating assets needed to support continued growth.

3.3 Common Size Statements (a.k.a. Vertical Analysis)

The next step in conducting a detailed analysis is to compare the financial statements of the proxy company to those of companies operating in the same industry. Our proxy company, Urban Outfitters, is a member of the retail apparel industry, which is part of the services sector.

One common method for identifying potential peers is through the use of Standard Industry Classification (SIC) codes, which are US government codes used to classify companies by type of business operation. Another common method involves the use of Reuters Industry Classification (RIC) codes. Both methods can be employed through the "screening tool" in MultexNet. The steps are provided below.

1. Launch MultexNet
2. Click the Screening Tool tab on the nav bar
3. In NetScreen Pro, click the "Add/Build" button. Under the Descriptive category, click "Industry Description" and click the "Select" button. The industry box will pop up. In the Industry box, check the radio button for the desired industry (e.g., retail apparel) and then click "Go." You will see the desired industry listed in the criterion box. Click "Go."
4. Click the hyperlink for the number of companies in the industry (e.g., 34). The report provides a list of companies in the industry. In the report, click the "Add/Remove/Arrange Columns" button. Under the Share Related Items Category, select "MktCap" and then click the ">" button to add market cap to your report.
5. In the report, click "Sort" and check the radio button to sort the data in descending order based on market cap. Click "Sort" to return to the report. The companies will now be listed in descending order of market cap (i.e., largest to smallest).

If you do not have access to MultexNet, a list of competitors can be obtained using Yahoo! Finance.

Comparing companies across an industry can be difficult for several reasons. For instance, the companies likely vary in size. In addition, the financial statements may be reported in different currencies – which require conversion – or the companies being compared may have different fiscal year ends. To standardize the financial statements of the proxy company and its peers, dollars ($) must be converted to percentages (%). The result is referred to as a common-size statement; see *Figures 3.2* and *3.3*.

Figure 3.2 Common Size Balance Sheet

Urban Outfitters, Inc.
Detailed Annual Balance Sheet

	As of 01/31/2003	As of 01/31/02	As of 01/31/01
ASSETS			
Cash/Equivalents	25.9%	14.5%	9.7%
Investments	2.7%	0.0%	0.2%
Accounts Rcvbl.	1.4%	2.4%	2.3%
Doubtful Account	-0.2%	-0.3%	-0.3%
Inventories	17.6%	21.1%	20.6%
Prepaids	3.1%	3.0%	4.3%
Deferred Taxes	1.6%	1.4%	1.7%
Total Current Assets	52.0%	42.1%	38.5%
Land	0.2%	0.3%	0.3%
Building	1.6%	2.2%	2.0%
Furnit./Fixtures	16.0%	18.4%	19.3%
Leasehold Imprv.	43.8%	55.0%	52.8%
Construction	1.3%	3.7%	4.3%
Prop. & Equip.	3.6%	4.1%	4.4%
Other Assets	3.2%	3.8%	3.5%
Depreciation	-27.3%	-29.7%	-25.2%
Investments	5.6%	0.0%	0.0%
Total Assets	100.0%	100.0%	100.0%
LIABILITIES & SHAREHOLDER EQUITY			
Accounts Payable	6.9%	10.7%	11.5%
Accrued Comp.	1.9%	2.0%	1.1%
Accrued Liabs.	6.7%	8.2%	7.2%
Total Current Liabs	15.5%	20.9%	19.7%
Long Term Debt	0.0%	0.0%	0.0%
Deferred Rent	3.8%	4.3%	3.4%
Total Liabilities	19.3%	25.2%	23.2%
Common Stock	0.0%	0.0%	0.0%
Paid in Capital	24.2%	9.2%	9.6%
Retained Earns.	56.3%	66.2%	67.6%
Total Equity	80.7%	74.8%	76.8%

To create a common size balance sheet, each item on the balance sheet must be expressed as a percentage of total assets or total liabilities and owner's equity. This conversion allows analysts to compare items on the balance sheet. For example, Urban Outfitters' inventory fell by 3.5% from 21.1% to 17.6% during 2003. Provided the company had enough inventory to meet customer demand, this would indicate that the company improved its inventory control measures. In addition, the company's current assets (52%) rose by 9.9 percent while current liabilities (15.5%) fell by 5.4 percent. Thus, we can assume that the company became more liquid during 2003.

Figure 3.3 Common Size Income Statement
Urban Outfitters, Inc.
Detailed Annual Income Statement (Thousands $)

	12 Months Ending 01/31/03	12 Months Ending 01/31/02	12 Months Ending 01/31/01
Total Revenue	100.0%	100.0%	100.0%
Cost of Sales	64.3%	67.4%	67.7%
Selling/Gen./Admin.	24.9%	25.3%	26.2%
Total Expenses	89.3%	92.7%	93.9%
Interest, Net	0.4%	0.1%	0.2%
Other, Net	-0.2%	-0.2%	-0.2%
Income Before Taxes	10.9%	7.2%	6.0%
Income Taxes	4.4%	2.9%	2.5%
Income After Taxes	6.5%	4.3%	3.6%

To standardize the income statement, each item on the income statement must be expressed as a percentage of total sales. This conversion tells us what happened to each dollar in sales. For example, taxes eat up $.04 of each dollar generated in sales. Selling, general, and administrative expenses account for another $0.24. In the end, approximately $0.06 of each dollar in sales flows through to the bottom line, and that entire amount is retained by the company; nothing is paid out shareholders.

The common size statements for any publicly-traded company in the US can be acquired through MultexNet. The steps involved are as follows:

1. Launch MultexNet
2. Enter the ticker symbol in the dialogue box
3. Click the radio button for "All Financial Statements"
4. Choose "Annual" from the drop down menu
5. Click the radio button for "Common Size" statements
6. Click "Go"

3.4 Ratio Analysis

Another way of comparing companies of different sizes is to calculate financial ratios. The ratios serve as a basis for determining the company's current financial position. At a basic level, the ratios for any company – public or private – can be divided into five categories: payout, financial strength, profitability, management effectiveness, and efficiency ratios. Each category is outlined below.

Financial Strength Ratios

The current ratio (sometimes referred to as the working capital ratio) is a measure of liquidity. To calculate the current ratio, current assets (i.e., cash, accounts receivable, inventory, etc.) are divided by current liabilities (i.e., accounts payable and other liabilities due in the next 12 months). In the case of Urban Outfitters, the current ratio for 2003 is 3.3568 ($144,584,000 / $43,072,000).

Equation 3.13

$$\text{Current Ratio} = \frac{\text{Current Assets}}{\text{Current Liabilities}}$$

Thus, we could say there is $3.36 in current assets for every $1 of current liabilities, or that Urban Outfitters has its current liabilities covered 3.36 times over. Given the fact that creditors lend money to a company with the promise of repayment, they prefer high current ratios that reflect liquidity. However, a high current ratio may also indicate an inefficient use of cash. For this reason, it is helpful to compare the company's current ratio to that of the industry; the ratio for the industry is 2.58. The high ratio in this case is likely a function of the company's expansion plans.

Figure 3.4 Industry Ratios

Ratio	URBN	Industry
Financial Strength Ratios		
1. Current Ratio	2.89	2.58
2. Quick Ratio	1.47	1.23
3. Debt to Equity Ratio	0.00	0.30
Profitability Ratio		
1. Gross Margin	38.93	36.00
2. Operating Margin	14.72	9.79
3. Net Profit Margin	8.82	6.16
Efficiency Ratios		
1. Receivables Turnover	96.57	42.62
2. Days' Sales in Receivables	3.78	8.56
3. Inventory Turnover	5.59	4.76
4. Days' Sales in Inventory	65.30	76.68
5. Asset Turnover	1.75	1.94
Management Effectiveness Ratios		
1. Return on Assets	15.46	11.48
2. Return on Equity	19.27	22.90

The ratios for the retail apparel industry are provided in *Figure 3.4*. Each ratio described in this section should be compared to the industry, which serves as a benchmark for company performance.

As noted in Chapter 2, assets are listed on the balance sheet in terms of decreasing liquidity. Inventory is often the least liquid current asset since items held in inventory must be sold in order to generate cash. More to the point, large inventories may be a sign that companies such as Urban Outfitters over bought. With the quick ratio (sometimes referred to as the acid test ratio), inventory is subtracted from current assets before dividing through by current liabilities. As a result, it provides a more accurate portrayal of the company's short-term liquidity.

Equation 3.14
$$\text{Quick Ratio} = \frac{\text{Current Assets} - \text{Inventory}}{\text{Current Liabilities}}$$

In the case of Urban Outfitters, inventory accounts for ⅓ of current assets. As such, the quick ratio is 2.23 [($144,584,000 - $48,825,000)/$43,072,000]. If the ratio is at least 1.0, the company has sufficient cash and accounts receivable to cover the liabilities that will come due in the next 12 months. In this case, the current liabilities are covered 2.23 times over.

Another measure of financial strength is the total debt ratio, which indicates the proportion of debt that a company has relative to assets. It is calculated by dividing total debt (i.e., total assets less total equity) by total assets. Urban Outfitters uses 19% debt ($53,611,000 / $277,996,000). Stated differently, the company has $.19 in debt for every $1 in assets. Therefore, Urban Outfitters has 81% (1.00 - 0.19) in equity. With this in mind, the debt-to-equity ratio is 0.23 (0.19 / 0.81).

Typically, a lower debt-to-equity ratio is favored, given the financial flexibility that accompanies it.

Equation 3.15

$$\text{Total Debt Ratio} = \frac{\text{Total Assets} - \text{Total Equity}}{\text{Total Assets}}$$

Equation 3.16

$$\text{Debt} - \text{Equity Ratio} = \frac{\text{Total Debt}}{\text{Total Equity}}$$

A measure of the company's ability to meet its obligations on outstanding liabilities is the interest coverage ratio (sometimes referred to as times interest earned or TIE). As the name suggests, the ratio measures how well a company is situated to cover its interest costs. Urban Outfitters has its interest costs covered 30.33 ($45,399,000 / $1,497,000) times over.

Equation 3.17

$$\text{Interest Coverage Ratio} = \frac{\text{EBIT}}{\text{Interest Expense}}$$

The problem with the interest coverage ratio is that it is based on EBIT, which does not accurately reflect the amount of cash available to pay interest charges since depreciation, a noncash expense, has been deducted. To overcome this problem, the cash coverage ratio can be used. Cash coverage, which adds back depreciation, is a basic measure of the company's ability to generate the cash needed to service its interest costs.

Equation 3.18

$$\text{Cash Coverage Ratio} = \frac{\text{EBIT} + \text{Depreciation}}{\text{Interest Expense}}$$

Efficiency Ratios

Efficiency ratios describe a company's ability to utilize assets to generate sales. Inventory turnover, for example, describes the number of times that a company turns over (or sells) its entire inventory during a twelve month period. In 2003, Urban Outfitters turned over its entire inventory 5.57 times ($271,963,000 / $48,825,000).

Equation 3.19

$$\text{Inventory Turnover} = \frac{\text{Cost of Goods Sold}}{\text{Inventory}}$$

As long as the company does not run out of inventory, the higher the ratio the better. By dividing 365 by the inventory turnover ratio, days' sales in inventory can be determined. On average, Urban Outfitters' inventory sits on the shelf for 65 days (365 / 5.57) before it is sold.

Equation 3.20

$$\text{Days' Sales in Inventory} = \frac{365 \text{ days}}{\text{Inventory Turnover}}$$

Inventory turnover gives us an indication of how long it takes a company to sells its various products. Receivables turnover, on the other hand, describes how quickly the company collects on those sales. In 2003, Urban Outfitters collected its outstanding credit accounts 110.52 times ($422,754,000 / $3,825,000). The quicker a company can collect on its receivables the better.

Equation 3.21

$$\text{Receivables Turnover} = \frac{\text{Sales}}{\text{Accounts Receivable}}$$

Using the days' sales in receivables ratio, we see that the company collects on credit sales every 3.30 days (365 / 110.52). This ratio is sometimes referred to as the average collection period.

Equation 3.22

$$\text{Days' Sales in Receivables} = \frac{365 \text{ days}}{\text{Receivables Turnover}}$$

Another efficiency ratio commonly used is total asset turnover, which provides a measure of the company's ability to turn assets into sales. For every dollar of assets, Urban Outfitters generated $1.52 (422,754,000 / $277,996,000) in sales in 2003. Obviously, the higher the ratio, the better.

Equation 3.23

$$\text{Total Asset Turnover} = \frac{\text{Sales}}{\text{Total Assets}}$$

Profitability Ratios

These ratios – gross margin, operating margin, and net profit margin – measure how efficiently a company manages its operations.

Gross margin is determined by dividing the difference between sales and cost of goods sold by sales. It indicates the percentage of net sales remaining after subtracting cost of goods sold.

Equation 3.24

$$\text{Gross Profit Margin} = \frac{(\text{Sales} - \text{Costs of Good Sold})}{\text{Sales}}$$

In the case of Urban Outfitters, the gross profit margin for 2003 is 0.36 [($422,754,000 - $271,963,000) / $422,754,000]. A high gross profit margin indicates that the company can generate a reasonable profit on sales, as long as other expenses are controlled.

Operating profit margin indicates how effective a company is at controlling the expenses associated with its normal business operations. It is calculated by dividing earnings before taxes (EBT) by sales. For Urban Outfitters, the operating profit margin for 2003 is 0.11 ($46,073,000 / $422,754,000). As a profitability measure, the higher the operating profit margin the better.

Equation 3.25

$$\text{Operating Profit Margin} = \frac{\text{Income Before Taxes}}{\text{Sales}}$$

The net profit margin (PM) provides a measure of a company's ability to generate profit. For 2003, Urban Outfitters generated $0.06 in profit for every $1 in sales ($27,413,000 / $422,754,000). A high profit margin is desirable since it indicates low expenses relative to sales.

Equation 3.26

$$\text{Net Profit Margin} = \frac{\text{Net Income}}{\text{Sales}}$$

Note: The profit margin is the same figure reported on the common size income statement.

Management Effectiveness Ratios

These ratios – return on assets and return on equity – measure management's effectiveness in using the company's assets or equity to generate profit.

Return on assets (ROA) is a measure of profit per dollar of assets. In 2003, Urban Outfitters had a ROA of 0.10 ($27,413,000 / $277,996,000). In other words, for every $1 in assets, the company generated $0.10 in profit.

Equation 3.27
$$\text{Return on Assets} = \frac{\text{Net Income}}{\text{Total Assets}}$$

As noted in Chapter 1, the goal of financial management is to create value for the owners of the company. Since equity is provided by the owners, return on equity (ROE) provides a measure of how those owners fared over the past twelve months. Urban Outfitters' 2003 ROE was 0.12 ($27,413,000 / $224,385,000). In other words, for every $1 of equity, the company generated $0.12 in profit. Although ROE varies by industry, most companies try to return at least 15 percent per year.

Equation 3.28
$$\text{Return on Equity} = \frac{\text{Net Income}}{\text{Total Equity}}$$

The ROA for Urban Outfitters is lower than the ROE (0.10 vs. 0.12). Is this customary? Actually, it is. The lower ratio reflects the fact that the company is using both debt and equity to finance its operations.

Payout Ratios

As noted in Chapter 2, net income can either be retained by the company or paid out to the owners in the form of dividends. The proportion of income paid out is referred to as the dividend payout ratio.

Equation 3.29

$$\text{Dividend Payout Ratio} = \frac{\text{Cash Dividend Per Share}}{\text{Earnings Per Share}}$$

Given the fact that Urban Outfitters does not pay dividends, the payout ratio is assumed to be zero. As a result, the retention ratio is 100 percent.

Equation 3.30

$$\text{Retention Ratio} = \frac{\text{Addition to Retained Earnings}}{\text{Net Income}}$$

Time Trend and Peer Group Analysis

Once the ratios have been calculated, there are two additional forms of analysis that can be completed: time trend and peer group analysis. With time trend analysis, the financial ratios of a single company are analyzed over several periods. For instance, the ratios for Urban Outfitters could be compared over the period extending from 2000 to 2003; see *Figure 3.5*.

Peer Group Analysis identifies firms that are similar in the sense that they compete in the same markets or operate in similar ways (a subjective assessment). Once the peer group has been identified, each ratio (e.g., current ratio) for the proxy company is compared to the peer group.

Figure 3.5 Time Trend Analysis

	01/31/03	01/31/02	01/31/01
Dividends			
Payout (or dividend) Rate	0.00	0.00	0.00
Retention Rate	1.00	1.00	1.00
Financial Strength			
Current Ratio	3.36	2.01	1.95
Quick (or Acid Test) Ratio	2.22	1.01	0.91
Profitability Ratios			
Gross Margin	0.36	0.33	0.32
Operating Margin	0.11	0.07	0.06
Profit Margin	0.06	0.04	0.04
Management Effectiveness			
Return on Assets	0.10	0.08	0.06
Return on Equity	0.12	0.10	0.08
Efficiency			
Receivables Turnover	110.52	74.39	74.88
Days Sales in Receivables	3.30	4.91	4.87
Inventory Turnover	5.57	5.73	5.75
Days Sales in Inventory	65.53	63.73	63.48
Asset Turnover	1.52	1.79	1.75

For example, the ratios for Urban Outfitters can be compared to Pacific Sunwear of California and Hot Topic; see *Figure 3.6*. The current ratio for Urban Outfitters exceeds the benchmark of 1.50, and is consistent with that of Hot Topic. The company's profit margin is the same as Pacific Sunwear, but lower than Hot Topic. As a measure of profitability, net profit margin provides a measure of management's ability to manage expenses. The return on equity for Urban Outfitters is less than the established benchmark (15 percent) and lower than that of both Pacific Sunwear and Hot Topic. Thus, when compared to its peer group, Urban Outfitters is not providing the same level of return to the company's owners.

Figure 3.6 Peer Group Analysis

Dividends	URBN	PSUN	HOTT
Financial Strength			
Current Ratio	3.36	2.49	3.77
Quick (or Acid Test) Ratio	2.22	0.32	2.50
Profitability Ratios			
Gross Margin	0.36	0.34	0.39
Operating Margin	0.11	0.10	0.13
Profit Margin	0.06	0.06	0.08
Management Effectiveness			
Return on Assets	0.10	0.12	0.20
Return on Equity	0.12	0.16	0.25
Efficiency			
Receivables Turnover	110.52	284.02	
Days Sales in Receivables	3.30	1.29	
Inventory Turnover	5.57	4.98	6.72
Days Sales in Inventory	65.53	73.38	54.31
Asset Turnover	1.52	2.12	2.43

END OF CHAPTER PROBLEMS

Questions and Problems
Chapter 3

1. Common size balance sheets are created by

   A. dividing balance sheet and income statement figures by total assets
   B. dividing asset accounts by total assets, liability accounts by total liabilities and equity accounts by total equity
   C. dividing accounts on the left hand side by total assets and accounts on the right hand side by total equity
   D. dividing all accounts by total assets minus total liabilities
   E. restating each item on the balance sheet as a percentage of total liabilities and owners equity

2. Costa's Hardware has total assets of $10,000,000 and a total asset turnover of 3.2 times. If the return on assets is 8 percent, what is Costa's profit margin?

   A. 2.50%
   B. 3.13%
   C. 3.19%
   D. 3.27%
   E. 3.34%

3. Four Corners Cleaners has a total debt ratio of 0.75, total debt of $150,000, and net income of $10,000. What is the company's return on equity?

   A. 0.10
   B. 0.20
   C. 0.30
   D. 0.40
   E. 0.50

Use the following information to answer the next 7 questions.

Williams Global Enterprises
2003 Income Statement
($ in millions)

Net Sales	1210
Less: Cost of Goods Sold	459
Less: Depreciation	264
EBIT	487
Less: Interest Paid	100
Taxable Income	387
Less: Taxes	122
Net Income	265
Addition to RE	?
Dividends Paid	?

Williams Global Enterprises
Balance Sheet as of 12/31/02 and 03
($ in millions)

Assets	2002	2003
Current Assets		
Cash	112	131
Accounts Receivable	361	311
Inventory	399	507
Total	872	949
Fixed Assets	1,701	1,963
Total Assets	2,573	2,912

Liabilities & Owners' Equity	2000	2001
Current Liabilities		
Accounts Payable	225	331
Notes Payable	411	305
Total	636	636
Long-term Debt	581	695
Equity	1,356	1,606
Total Liabilities and Equity	2,573	2,937

4. What was Williams Global's Operating Cash Flow in 2003?

   A. $101
   B. $629
   C. $873
   D. $912

5. How much did Williams Global pay to its shareholders in dividends in 2003?

   A. $15
   B. $125
   C. $250
   D. $265

6. What was the company's primary use of cash during 2003?

   A. Accounts Receivable
   B. Inventory
   C. Fixed Assets
   D. Long-term Debt

7. Did the company become more or less liquid during 2002?

   A. Less
   B. More
   C. Not enough information
   D. I do not know

8. What was the quick ratio in 2003?

    A. 1.49
    B. 0.90
    C. 0.70
    D. 0.57

9. What was the return on equity in 2003?

    A. 16.00%
    B. 16.50%
    C. 17.00%
    D. 17.50%

10. What was Williams Global's average tax rate in 2003?

    A. 31.52%
    B. 34.00%
    C. 39.00%
    D. 46.04%

CASE STUDY

Detailed Financial Analysis
Case 3.1

Using the financial statement data for Pacific Sunwear, create a common size income statement and balance sheet using the template provided.

Pacific Sunwear of California
Detailed Annual Income Statement
(Thousands of U.S. Dollars)

	12 Months Ending 01/31/03	12 Months Ending 01/31/02	12 Months Ending 01/31/2001
Net Sales			
Cost of Sales			
Selling/Gen./Admin.			
Total Expenses			
Interest, Net			
Other, Net			
Income Before Taxes			
Income Taxes			
Income After Taxes			

Based on your analysis, how would you characterize the profitability of this company? Your response should include an analysis of the current year as well as any discernable trends over the past three years. Has the company become more or less efficient? Based on your analysis, how would you describe the company's liquidity position?

Pacific Sunwear of California
Detailed Annual Balance Sheet (Thousands $)

	As of 01/31/2003	As of 01/31/2002	As of 01/31/2001
ASSETS			
Cash/Equivalents			
Investments			
Accounts Rcvbl.			
Doubtful Account			
Inventories			
Prepaids			
Deferred Taxes			
Total Current Assets			
Land			
Building			
Furnit./Fixtures			
Leasehold Imprv.			
Construction			
Prop. & Equip.			
Other Assets			
Depreciation			
Investments			
Total Assets			
LIABILITIES & OE			
Accounts Payable			
Accrued Comp.			
Accrued Liabs.			
Total Current Liabs			
Long Term Debt			
Deferred Rent			
Total Liabilities			
Common Stock			
Paid in Capital			
Retained Earns.			
Total Equity			

Pacific Sunwear of California

	As of 01/31/03	As of 01/31/02	Change	Source/Use
ASSETS				
Cash/Equivalents	36,438	23,136		
Accounts Rcvbl.	2,916	3,044		
Inventories	123,433	102,512		
Prepaids	14,871	11,856		
Deferred Taxes	4,975	4,282		
Total Current Assets	182,633	144,830		
Land	12,156	12,156		
Buildings	26,680	26,475		
Leashold	111,431	102,075		
Furniture	148,377	125,706		
Depreciation	-97,131	-71,412		
Goodwill	0	8,100		
Deposits/Other	9,105	7,807		
Deferred Taxes	0	1,311		
Total Asset	399,743	355,440		
LIABILITIES & OE				
Notes Payable	829	425		
Accounts Payable	28,456	37,493		
Accrued Liabs.	34,522	17,743		
Cur. Port. LT Debt	1,521	834		
Income Taxes	8,000	9,436		
Total Current Liabs	73,328	65,931		
Long Term Debt	1,102	24,597		
Capital Leases	2,236	731		
Deferred Taxes	3,015	0		
Deferred Comp	7,097	7,439		
Deferred Rent	10,574	8,759		
Total Liabilities	97,352	107,485		
Common Stock	495	492		
Paid in Capital	93,008	88,252		
Retained Earns.	208,888	159,211		
Total Equity	302,391	247,955		

Using the financial statement data, construct a Sources and Uses of Cash Statement for Pacific Sunwear using the template provided above. Based on your analysis, what was the company's primary sources and uses of cash?

Complete a thorough ratio analysis for Pacific Sunwear. The analysis should include the calculation and interpretation of each ratio listed below.

	02/01/03	Interpretations:
Payout Ratios Payout (or dividend) Rate Retention Rate		
Financial Strength Current Ratio Quick (or Acid Test) Ratio Debt-to-Equity		
Profitability Ratios Gross Margin Operating Margin Profit Margin		
Management Effectiveness Return on Assets Return on Equity		
Efficiency Receivables Turnover Days' Sales in Receivables Inventory Turnover Days' Sales in Inventory Asset Turnover		

CHAPTER 4
FINANCIAL FORECASTING

Learning Objectives

After reading this chapter, you should be able to answer the following questions:

1. What is meant by the financial planning process? What is the difference between long- and short-range financial plans?
2. What is the purpose of the cash budget? How can the cash budget be used to determine the firm's short-term borrowing and investment requirements?
3. What is the key input required for preparing pro forma statements using the percentage of sales approach?
4. Briefly describe the pro forma income statement preparation process using the percentage-of-sales method. What is the driving force behind this model? What are the strengths and weaknesses of this approach?
5. Describe the judgmental approach used to prepare a pro forma balance sheet. What is the significance of the "plug figure," external financing required? What are the ramifications of a positive plug figure? What about a negative plug figure?

A lack of long-range planning is a commonly cited reason for financial distress and bankruptcy. Financial planning is the process of forecasting a company's future growth. Value is created on the left-hand side of the balance sheet when companies make good investments (i.e., capital budgeting) that ultimately increase operating cash flows. How companies finance those investments (i.e., capital structure) on the right-hand side of the balance sheet – whether through debt, equity, or retained earnings – is also critical. In this chapter, we will explore how financial planning and forecasting can be used to better understand the growth potential of companies of varying sizes.

4.1 Financial Planning Process

The financial planning process begins with long-term, strategic plans that direct the formation of short-term, operating plans and cash budgets. Long-term plans outline the company's planned activities for a period of two to ten years. These plans, along with production and marketing plans, provide the framework for achieving a company's strategic objectives. Short-term plans, on the other hand, detail the company's short-term business activities. Typically, these plans – which are outlined in this chapter – address the next period or two, and include the cash budget and pro forma financial statements.

Short-term financial planning begins with the generation of a sales forecast, which is provided by the Marketing Department. With the sales forecast, a production plan – with estimates of the necessary raw materials, labor, and overhead – can be devised. The production plan is developed by the Vice President for Operations (COO) and other operations management specialists. Next, the company constructs a pro forma income statement and cash budget. By combining these reports with the current period balance sheet and fixed asset outlay plan, the company has the necessary inputs to construct the pro forma balance sheet. The short-term financial planning process is illustrated in *Figure 4.1*.

4.2 Cash Budget

The cash budget is a statement of the company's planned inflows and outflows of cash over a fixed period of time. Generally, the cash budget provides information for a one-year period on either a monthly or quarterly basis. The more seasonal and uncertain the company's cash flow patterns, the higher the likelihood that the data will be provided on a monthly basis. For retail apparel companies like Urban Outfitters, which are exposed to seasonal fluctuations in revenue and expenses, a monthly cash budget is required. The cash budget is used to estimate the company's short-term cash requirements. If the company expects a cash shortfall, then arrangements can be made to acquire short-term financing (e.g., notes payable). If, on the other hand, the company expects a cash surplus, the additional funds can be invested (e.g. marketable securities) to generate a return.

Figure 4.1 Short-term Planning Process

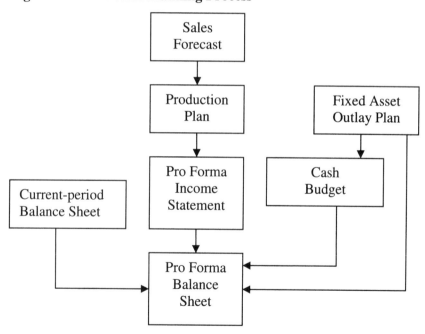

As noted in *Figure 4.1*, the key input to the short-term financial planning process is the sales forecast. The forecast is typically provided to the financial manager by the Marketing Department. In constructing the forecast, the marketing department uses both primary and secondary market data to estimate the company's monthly sales receipts (i.e., units sold x selling price). With the assistance of operations, the financial manager can then approximate the monthly operating expenses incurred to generate those sales (i.e., cost of goods sold). Operations will also provide critical input regarding the amount of fixed assets required to support the level of sales.

Figure 4.2 Cash Budget (Thousands $)

	October	November	December
Cash receipts	$175	$290	$470
Less: Cash disbursements	$197	$346	$371
Net cash flow	($22)	($56)	$99
Plus: Beginning cash	$50	$27	($29)
Ending cash	$28	($29)	$70
Less: Minimum cash balance	$20	$20	$20
Financing required	$0	$49	$0
Excess cash balance	$8	$0	$50

The typical format for a cash budget is presented in *Figure 4.2*. To construct the cash budget, we begin by subtracting cash disbursements from cash receipts. Cash receipts represent all of the company's cash inflows for a given period, which are divided into three categories: cash sales, accounts receivable, and other; see *Figure 4.3*. Other cash receipts include all expected sources of cash other than sales, such as interest income, dividend income, and the proceeds received on the sale of real assets (e.g., equipment) or financial assets (e.g., stocks and bonds).

As illustrated in *Figure 4.4*, cash disbursements represent all cash outlays during the same period, including wages, rent, principal and interest payments, dividend payments, and tax payments. The excess cash balance of $8,000 in October and $50,000 in December can be invested in marketable securities. The cash shortfall in November ($49,000) will need to be financed. Typically, these shortages are financed through the sale of the marketable securities purchased in October.

Figure 4.3 Cash Receipts (Thousands $)

	October	November	December
Cash sales	$25	$50	$100
Collection of AR			
0 – 30 days	$100	$180	$240
30 – 60 days	$50	$60	$90
Other cash receipts	$0	$0	$40
Total cash receipts	$175	$290	$470

Figure 4.4 Cash Disbursements

	October	November	December
Cash purchases	$35	$28	$21
Payment of:			
Accounts payable			
0 – 30 days	$100	$90	$150
30 – 60 days	$21	$42	$84
Rent	$5	$5	$5
Wages, salaries, etc.	$21	$31	$41
Principal	$0	$0	$30
Interest	$0	$0	$10
Stock repurchases	$0	$0	$0
Dividends	$15	$0	$0
Taxes	$0	$0	$30
Acquisition of fixed assets	$0	$150	$0
Total cash disbursements	$197	$346	$371

If the sale proceeds are insufficient to cover the cash shortfall, then short-term borrowing (e.g., notes payable) would be required. For instance, the financial manager could establish a line of credit with a commercial bank. A line of credit is loan that can be used as needed to cover ongoing operating expenses. In this case, a line of credit for $10,000 should be sufficient.

4.3 Growth Potential

Before constructing projected financial statements, management must have an understanding of the company's growth potential. Using three of the financial ratios outlined in Chapter 3 – plowback ratio (i.e., retention ratio), return on assets, and return on equity – we can determine the internal growth rate and sustainable growth rate for a company. The internal growth rate is the rate attainable through the use of internal financing only. Sustainable growth rate, on the other hand, is the rate achievable if the company maintains a constant debt ratio.

Internal Growth Rate

As noted in Chapter 2, net income can either be retained by the company or paid out to the owners in the form of a dividend. The proportion of income paid out is referred to as the dividend payout ratio. Given the fact that Urban Outfitters does not pay dividends, the payout ratio is assumed to be zero. As a result, the retention ratio is 100 percent.

Return on Assets (ROA) provides a measure of the income generated by the company's assets, and as such, is calculated by dividing net income by total assets. The 2003 ROA for Urban Outfitters is 0.10 ($27,413,000 / $277,996,000). Thus, for every $1 in assets, the company generates $0.10 in profit. Using ROA and the plowback ratio, we can determine the internal growth rate; that is, the growth rate that can be achieved using internal funds only.

Equation 4.1
Internal Growth Rate = ROA × b

$$= .010 \times 1.00 = 0.10$$

The internal growth rate for Urban Outfitters is .10. Thus, the company can achieve a growth rate of 10 percent without having to raise funds (i.e., debt and equity) through the capital markets.

Sustainable Growth Rate

Return on equity (ROE) provides a measure of how the owners of the company fared over the past twelve months. It is calculated by dividing total equity into net income. Urban Outfitters' 2003 ROE was 0.12 ($27,413,000 / $224,385,000). In other words, for every $1 of equity, the company generated $0.12 in profit. By combining the retention ratio with ROE, the company's sustainable growth rate can be determined. Given the 100 percent retention rate, the 2003 sustainable growth rate for Urban Outfitters will be the same as the return on equity (12 percent). In other words, the company can expect to grow by 12 percent by maintaining the same debt ratio of 19 percent.

Equation 4.2
Sustainable Growth Rate = ROE × b

$$= 0.12 \times 1.00 = 0.12$$

Generally, it is advantageous for a company to maintain (or preferably decrease) its debt ratio. By issuing new equity (e.g., stock), the income generated by the company will be spread over a larger number of shares. Therefore, the existing owners' interest becomes diluted. In addition, the earnings per share (net income / shares outstanding) reported by the company will decline, even if the income generated next period remains constant.

4.4 Pro Forma Financial Statements

Pro forma financial statements are used in two important ways to create value. First, the statements are used to estimate future free cash flow, which enables management to measure the firm's current value, and, more importantly, to investigate the impact of proposed changes in strategy on the company's future value. Second, the statements are needed to forecast the financing that will be required to execute the company's operating plans. For instance, Urban Outfitters may want to achieve a 15 percent growth rate. As noted above, the company can expect to achieve a growth rate of 10 percent using internally generated funds. The question, therefore, is: How much external funding will be needed for the company to meet its desired growth rate of 15 percent? In this section, we will explore the various methods used to construct projected financial statements and determine the amount of external funds needed.

Percentage of Sales Approach

The percentage of sales approach is the most common method used to construct a pro forma income statement. Two inputs are needed: (1) the income statement for the preceding year and (2) the sales forecast for the coming year. Just as with the cash budget, the driving force in this model is the sales forecast. Once the percentage increase in sales is determined, most of the other values in the pro forma statement are calculated based on it. For the purpose of this example, we will assume a projected growth rate in sales of 15 percent (when compared to 2003).

To construct a pro forma income statement, we must determine the ratio of costs to sales for each item listed on the income statement. The ratios are then multiplied by the 2004 sales forecast to determine the 2004 costs. For instance, since the costs of goods sold represent 64.33 percent of sales ($271,963,000 / $422,754,000) in 2003, this same percentage would be multiplied by the sales forecast for 2004 to estimate the costs of goods sold for 2004 ($312,757). Likewise, total expenses represent 89.26 percent of sales ($377,355,000 / $422,754,000). 89.26 percent of $486,167,000 is $433,958,000. This figure will be used as an estimate of total expenses for 2004.

Interest expense is held constant (since long-term debt on the pro forma balance sheet remains unchanged). The retention rate – that is, the percentage of income retained by the company – is also held constant. For example, if the company had paid out 20 percent of income to shareholders in the form of dividends in 2003, that same percentage would be assumed to be paid out in 2004. In the case of Urban Outfitters, the dividend payout ratio is 0, so all of the after-tax income ($31,464,000) flows through to the balance sheet as an addition to retained earnings; see *Figure 4.5*.

With the percentage of sales approach, all expenses are assumed to be variable. If we were to examine operating expenses, however, we would find that they are comprised of both fixed (rent) and variable (utilities) expenses. As a result, the use of the percentage of sales approach – and past expense ratios – tends to overstate profits when sales are decreasing and understate profits when sales are increasing. The reason is simple: if a company has fixed costs, these costs do not change when sales increase; the result is increased profits. By remaining unchanged when sales decline, these costs tend to reduce earnings. To prevent this problem when constructing a pro forma income statement, the company's historical costs should be divided into fixed and variable components whenever possible.

Figure 4.5 Pro Forma Income Statement

Urban Outfitters, Inc.
Detailed Annual Income Statement
(Thousands $)

	12 Months Ending 01/31/03	12 Months Ending 01/31/04	
Total Revenue	$ 422,754	$ 486,167	
Cost of Sales	$ 271,963	$ 312,751	64.33%
Selling/Gen./Admin.	$ 105,392	$ 121,201	24.93%
Total Expenses	$ 377,355	$ 433,952	89.26%
Interest, Net	$ 1,497	$ 1,497	
Other, Net	$ (823)	$ (823)	
Income Before Taxes	$ 46,073	$ 52,883	
Income Taxes	$ 18,660	$ 21,418	40.5%
Income After Taxes	$ 27,413	$ 31,465	
Dividend Yield	0%	0%	
Retention Rate	100%	100%	
Additions to RE	$ 27,413	$ 31,465	

Judgmental Approach

The judgmental (or subjective) approach is the most common method used in constructing a pro forma balance sheet and determining external funds needed (EFN). Like the income statement, assets are increased by the percentage increase in sales. After all, additional assets are needed to support the projected increase in sales. Those liabilities (e.g., accounts payable) directly related to sales are also increased. Other liabilities (e.g., long-term debt) and equity are held constant. Intuitively, this should make sense. After all, we are trying to determine the amount of debt and equity needed to fund the projected increase in sales.

Financial Management: A Practical Guide to Value Creation   109

Figure 4.6 Pro Forma Balance Sheet
Urban Outfitters, Inc.
Detailed Annual Income Statement (Thousands $)

	As of 01/31/03		As of 01/31/04	
ASSETS				
Cash/Equivalents	$	72,127		
Investments	$	7,379		
Accounts Rcvbl.	$	3,825		
Doubtful Account	$	(563)		
Inventories	$	48,825		
Prepaids	$	8,633		
Deferred Taxes	$	4,358		
Total Current Assets	$	144,584		
Land	$	543		
Building	$	4,331		
Furnit./Fixtures	$	44,487		
Leasehold Imprv.	$	121,878		
Construction	$	3,487		
Prop. & Equip.	$	10,056		
Other Assets	$	8,925		
Depreciation	$	(75,935)		
Investments	$	15,640		
Total Assets	$	277,996	$ 319,695	(+ 15%)
LIABILITIES & SHAREHOLDER EQUITY				
Accounts Payable	$	19,186	$ 22,064	(+ 15%)
Accrued Comp.	$	5,197	$ 5,977	(+ 15%)
Accrued Liabs.	$	18,689	$ 21,492	(+ 15%)
Total Current Liabs	$	43,072	$ 49,533	(+ 15%)
Long Term Debt	$	-		
Deferred Rent	$	10,539	$ 10,539	
Common Stock	$	2	$ 2	
Paid in Capital	$	67,162	$ 67,162	
Retained Earns.	$	156,529	$ 187,994	+ $31,465
Other Comp.	$	692	$ 692	
Total Liabilities and SO	$	277,996	$ 315,922	
EXTERNAL FUNDS NEEDED			$ 3,773	

Retained earnings, on the other hand, is increased by the "addition to retained earnings" calculated on the pro forma income statement.

Determining the external financing needed is a two step process: create pro forma balance sheet for the next period, then calculate the difference between total assets and total liabilities and shareholder equity. As noted in Chapter 2, the balance sheet sets assets equal to liabilities and shareholder equity. However, the pro forma financial statement created for FY 2004 does not balance; see *Figure 4.6*. Total assets equal $319,695,000 while the liabilities and owners' equity total $315,922,000. The difference of $3,773,000 represents the external funds needed to meet the company's growth projections and bring the balance sheet into balance. Note: With the judgmental approach, economic assumptions (e.g., interest rates, inflation rates, tax rates, etc.) and corporate policies can also be reflected in the analysis. For instance, if the company estimates that it takes 70 days to satisfy accounts payable, then accounts payable should be forecasted as 1/5 (70 / 360) of the company's purchases.

If the external financing needed is a positive value, then the company must raise funds externally to support operations. Should the additional funding be debt or equity? Debt is typically less costly than equity, but requires fixed payments of principal and interest. The company's debt ratio is .19. Since the company's debt ratio is lower than that of the industry and debt is typically less costly than equity, it would be the likely choice for Urban Outfitters. Once the form of financing is determined, the pro forma balance sheet would be modified to reflect the planned increase in either debt or equity. If the value had been negative, on the other hand, the company would have excess cash flow. In that case, funds would be available to increase dividend payments to the owners of the company, repurchase company stock, and so on. Again, once the specific use for the excess funds is determined, the pro forma balance sheet would be updated.

The same financial analysis – sources and uses of cash, financial ratios, and free cash flow – outlined in Chapter 3 can be applied to the pro forma financial statements. By doing so, the ramifications of the management's proposed activities can be better understood.

APPENDIX 4.1 PRO FORMA FINANCIAL STATEMENTS

In many cases, you will be asked to construct a sales forecast, pro forma financial statements, or both. The accuracy of these forecasts can be greatly improved through the use of Crystal Ball Professional. Crystal Ball Professional is a software suite comprised of three components: CB Predictor, Crystal Ball, and OptQuest. CB Predictor allows the user to exploit time series data (i.e., historical data) to forecast future periods. This application is very useful in constructing sales forecasts when relevant historical information is available.

Forecasting Units Sold

A retail apparel company is interested in constructing a pro forma income statement. The monthly sales data for the period extending from 09/30/92 to 07/31/01 is provided below. This information can be used to forecast the next 12 months of sales (08/30/01 – 07/31/02). To do so:

1. Launch Crystal Ball
2. Open the file
3. Highlight the cells containing the data range and historical sales data
4. Click "CB Tools" and "CB Predictor"
5. There are four folder tabs on the *CB Predictor* dialog box: Input Data, Data Attributes, Method Gallery, and Results. The input folder requires that you identify the cell range for the data series. It also requires that you identify how the data is arranged. In this case, the monthly sales data is arranged in columns. Check the appropriate radio button and click "Next".
6. In the data attributes folder, you must indicate the format of the data. *CB Predictor* can accommodate data in seconds, minutes, hours, days, weeks, months, and years. Click the drop-down menu and choose "Months". You also have the opportunity to build seasonality into the forecast. Since we are examining the monthly

sales data for a retail apparel company, seasonality is important. The seasonality range should be set to "monthly." Be sure that the "Use Multiple Linear Regression" box is not checked and click "Next".

7. The Methods Gallery offers up to eight different methods for forecasting seasonal and nonseasonal times series data. The basic difference between the non-seasonal (left) and seasonal (right) methods is that the non-seasonal method estimates a smooth trend for the forecast by removing extreme data points. By contract, the seasonal methods permit the peaks and troughs encountered throughout the year. For a retail apparel company with sales that vary by month, it is important to reflect seasonality. Check all of the seasonal methods and click "Next".

8. The Results folder allows you to customize the output of for the forecasted data. In this case, the data should be forecasted for 12 periods, and a 5% - 95% level of confidence must be used. Check the Report radio button and label the report "Forecasted Sales." Then, click "Run".

The forecasted sales for the next 12 months will be added to your spreadsheet model. In addition, the CB Predictor Report will be created and saved in a worksheet labeled "Report." Both the model and the report are provided in *Figure A41.1*.

Constructing Pro Forma Financial Statements

Using Historical Data

With the sales forecast complete, the next step is to construct a pro forma income statement. The company's historical expenses can be used as a guideline. Each cost should be restated as a percentage of sales. In this case, the past ten years of financial statement data were used. *Figure A41.2* illustrates the calculations for the two most recent years. Ignoring taxes (which will be calculated at the marginal rate of 34 percent), the

114   CHAPTER 4 Financial Forecasting

company has three expenses: costs of goods sold, operating expenses, and interest expense. These expenses were restated as a percentage of net sales. Using these percentages, a minimum, maximum, and most likely value can be determined and used as assumption cells; see *Figure A41.3*.

Figure A41.1 Sales Forecast

Sales Forecast:

Date	Lower: 5%	Forecast	Upper: 95%
08/30/01	$1,426	$1,553	$1,681
09/29/01	$1,549	$1,677	$1,806
10/30/01	$1,126	$1,256	$1,385
11/29/01	$1,315	$1,446	$1,577
12/30/01	$2,672	$2,804	$2,937
01/29/02	$777	$910	$1,044
03/01/02	$768	$903	$1,038
03/31/02	$1,352	$1,489	$1,625
04/30/02	$1,087	$1,224	$1,362
05/31/02	$1,049	$1,188	$1,327
06/30/02	$1,330	$1,471	$1,611
07/31/02	$928	$1,070	$1,212

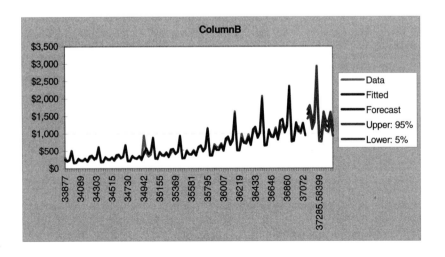

Financial Management: A Practical Guide to Value Creation   115

Month	Sales	Month	Sales	Month	Sales
9/30/1992	$315	2/29/1996	$270	4/30/1999	$740
10/31/1992	$211	3/31/1996	$473	5/31/1999	$780
11/30/1992	$251	4/30/1996	$370	6/30/1999	$977
12/31/1992	$521	5/31/1996	$358	7/31/1999	$696
1/31/1993	$158	6/30/1996	$439	8/31/1999	$1,029
2/28/1993	$165	7/31/1996	$323	9/30/1999	$1,119
3/31/1993	$250	8/31/1996	$441	10/31/1999	$897
4/30/1993	$229	9/30/1996	$529	11/30/1999	$1,065
5/31/1993	$218	7/31/1996	$323	12/31/1999	$2,075
6/30/1993	$276	8/31/1996	$441	1/31/2000	$719
7/31/1993	$199	9/30/1996	$529	2/29/2000	$696
8/31/1993	$291	10/31/1996	$413	3/31/2000	$1,070
9/30/1993	$350	11/30/1996	$484	4/30/2000	$966
10/31/1993	$257	12/31/1996	$896	5/31/2000	$930
11/30/1993	$290	1/31/1997	$288	6/30/2000	$1,170
12/31/1993	$593	2/28/1997	$304	7/31/2000	$851
1/31/1994	$177	3/31/1997	$524	8/31/2000	$1,090
2/28/1994	$185	4/30/1997	$403	9/30/2000	$1,250
3/31/1994	$316	5/31/1997	$413	10/31/2000	$1,070
4/30/1994	$251	6/30/1997	$532	11/30/2000	$1,280
5/31/1994	$242	7/31/1997	$400	12/31/2000	$2,360
6/30/1994	$308	8/31/1997	$597	1/31/2001	$938
7/31/1994	$223	9/30/1997	$648	2/28/2001	$784
8/31/1994	$309	10/31/1997	$521	3/31/2001	$1,200
10/31/1994	$293	12/31/1997	$1,160	5/31/2001	$1,000
11/30/1994	$332	1/31/1998	$384	6/30/2001	$1,300
12/31/1994	$665	2/28/1998	$414	7/31/2001	$948
1/31/1995	$213	3/31/1998	$693	**08/30/01**	**$1,553**
2/28/1995	$209	4/30/1998	$613	**09/29/01**	**$1,677**
3/31/1995	$340	5/31/1998	$609	**10/30/01**	**$1,256**
4/30/1995	$300	6/30/1998	$724	**11/29/01**	**$1,446**
5/31/1995	$276	7/31/1998	$572	**12/30/01**	**$2,804**
6/30/1995	$347	8/31/1998	$795	**01/29/02**	**$910**
7/31/1995	$245	9/30/1998	$874	**03/01/02**	**$903**
8/31/1995	$945	10/31/1998	$731	**03/31/02**	**$1,489**
9/30/1995	$467	11/30/1998	$868	**04/30/02**	**$1,224**
10/31/1995	$344	12/31/1998	$1,634	**05/31/02**	**$1,188**
11/30/1995	$396	1/31/1999	$528	**06/30/02**	**$1,471**
12/31/1995	$811	2/28/1999	$548	**07/31/02**	**$1,070**

Figure A41.2 Historical Income Statement
Detailed Annual Income Statement
(Thousands of U.S. Dollars)

	52 Weeks Ending 02/03/01	% of Sales	52 Weeks Ending 01/29/00	% of Sales
Net Sales	$13,673,460		$11,635,398	
Cost of Good Sold	$8,599,442	62.89%	$6,775,262	58.23%
Gross Profit	$5,074,018		$4,860,136	
Operating Expense	$3,629,257	26.54%	$3,043,432	26.16%
Interest Expense	$74,891		$44,966	
Interest Income	-$12,015		-$13,211	
Interest, Net	$0		$0	
Earnings Before Taxes	$1,381,885		$1,784,949	
Income Taxes	$504,388		$657,884	
Net Earnings	$877,497		$1,127,065	
Interest	$62,876	0.46%	$31,755	0.27%

Figure A41.3 Statistical Parameters

Expense	Minimum	Maximum	Mode
Costs of Goods Sold	58.23%	66.06%	62.55%
Operating Expense	22.34%	26.54%	24.14%
Interest Expense	-0.37%	0.46%	0.03%

Integrating Crystal Ball

Crystal Ball is a simulation tool used in forecasting unknown variables such as income and earnings per share, and as such, can be used in constructing pro forma financial statements. Simulation is an analytical method used to imitate a real-life system through a spreadsheet model. After constructing the model, probability distributions are used to define the possible outcomes for each input variable (or cell) in the spreadsheet. Then, by repeatedly sampling values for each variable, the program calculates hundreds - or even thousands - of possible outcomes in a few seconds. Through simulation, Crystal Ball extends the forecasting capabilities of MS Excel and provides the information needed to make accurate, efficient, and confident business decisions.

In Crystal Ball, a probability distribution can be used to describe the data in each assumption cell. To accomplish this, select from the 17 distribution types in the Distribution Gallery. Choosing the appropriate distribution can be challenging. Provided below is an outline of the most commonly used distributions.

1. Uniform Distribution - Used in situations where all values between the minimum and maximum values are equally likely to occur.
2. Triangular Distribution – Used in situations where the minimum, maximum, and most likely outcome are known.
3. Normal Distribution – Used when the mean and standard deviation for a particular input is given.

To apply an assumption using Crystal Ball, simply:

1. Select the cell
2. Click "Cell" and "Define Assumption"
3. From the distribution gallery, choose the appropriate probability distribution (e.g., normal distribution)
4. Enter the information necessary to define the distribution (e.g., mean and standard deviation)
5. Click "OK"

Figure A41.4 Assumption Cells
Assumptions

Cost of Good Sold	**62.55%**
Operating Expenses	**24.14%**
Interest	**0.03%**
Taxes	36.50%
Shares Outstanding	853,996,980

Assigning a forecast means selecting a cell with a numerical equation and requesting that Crystal Ball capture its output results from the simulation. In this case, the cell containing the formula for earnings per share (EPS) will be the forecast cell.

To apply the forecast:

1. Select the appropriate cell
2. Click "Cell" and "Define Forecast"
3. Enter the name of the cell (e.g., NPV) and the units (e.g., US Dollars)
4. Click "OK"

Before running the simulation, you must set the run preferences as follows:

1. Click "Run" and "Run Preferences"
2. Click the "Trials" button
3. Set the maximum number of trials to 5,000
4. Click the "Sampling" button
5. Uncheck the Random Number Generation radio button

6. Set the sampling method to Latin hypercube by clicking the appropriate radio button. During the simulation, *Crystal Ball 2000* will randomly choose values for each assumption cell using the parameters inputed. There are two sampling methods: Monte Carlo and Latin hypercube. With Monte Carlo, random numbers are generated that are completely independent of one another. With Latin hypercube sampling, *Crystal Ball 2000* divides the assumption's probability distribution into segments of equal probability. Then, the program generates random numbers for each segment. This method ensures that the entire distribution is represented in the simulation, thereby allowing users to generate better results with fewer trials.
7. Click "OK"

To run the simulation, click "Run" and "Run". The output for the forecast statistic will be captured in the frequency chart throughout the simulation. It can also be viewed on screen by clicking "View" and "Statistics". The results of the simulation can either be exported or included in a report. In this case, the simulation indicates that the company will receive $1,432,864,906 in income next year. The company's earning per share is estimated to be $1.68; see *Figure A41.5*.

Figure A41.5 Forecast Statistics

	Total
Net Sales	$16,991,567,525
Cost of Good Sold	$10,628,225,487
Gross Profit	$6,363,342,038
Operating Expenses	$4,101,764,400
Interest	$5,097,470
Earnings Before Taxes	$2,256,480,167
Income Taxes	$823,615,261
Net Earnings	$1,432,864,906
Earnings per Share (EPS)	$1.68

To create a report:

1. Click "Run" and "Create Report"
2. Click the radio buttons for the desired output
3. Click "OK"

To extract the data:

1. Click "Run" and "Extract Data"
2. Click the radio buttons for the desired output
3. Click "OK"

END OF CHAPTER PROBLEMS

Questions and Problems
Chapter 4

1. When using the percentage of sales approach to calculate the external funds needed, all items on the income statement directly related to sales are:

   A. Increased
   B. Decreased
   C. Increased and then decreased
   D. Held constant
   E. None of the above

2. When using the percentage of sales approach to calculate external funds needed, the payout ratio is:

   A. Increased
   B. Decreased
   C. Increased and then decreased
   D. Held constant
   E. None of the above

3. What is the most common method used to calculate the pro forma balance sheet?

   A. Percentage of Sales Approach
   B. Judgmental Approach
   C. Percentage of Assets Approach
   D. Historical Value Approach

4. _____ is a statement of the company's planned inflows and outflows of cash over a fixed period of time.

   A. Income Statement
   B. Statement of Cash Flows
   C. Cash Budget
   D. Balance Sheet

Use the following information to answer the next 6 questions.

Income Statement

Sales	$1,000
Costs	800
Taxable Income	$ 200
Taxes	68
Net Income	$ 132
Dividends	$ 44

Balance Sheet

Assets		Liabilities and Owners Equity	
Current Assets		Current Liabilities	
Cash	$ 160	Accounts Payable	$ 300
Accounts Receivable	440	Notes Payable	100
Inventory	600	Total	$ 400
Total	$1,200		
		Long-term Debt	$ 800
Fixed Assets	$1,800		
		Owners' Equity	
		Common Stock	$ 800
		Retained Earnings	1,000
		Total	$1,800
Total Assets	$3,000	Total Liabilities &OE	$3,000

5. What is the addition to retained earning for the current year?

   A. $0
   B. $44
   C. $88
   D. $132
   E. None of the above

6. The company has projected a 25 percent increase in sales for the coming year. Based on the percentage of sales approach, what is pro forma net income for the coming year?

   A. $0
   B. $132
   C. $150
   D. $165
   E. None of the above

7. Based on the percentage of sales approach, the dividends paid in the coming year will be _____?

   A. $0
   B. $44
   C. $55
   D. $132
   E. $165

8. Based on the percentage of judgmental approach, the retained earnings in the coming year will be _____?

   A. $0
   B. $1,000
   C. $1,110
   D. $1,200
   E. $1,500

9. Based on the judgmental approach, external funds needed will be?

   A. $0
   B. $235
   C. $375
   D. $565
   E. $967

10. What would be the most appropriate funding source?

    A. Common stock
    B. Preferred stock
    C. Long-term debt
    D. Retained earnings
    E. It cannot be determined

CASE ANALYSIS

Long–term Planning
Case 4.1

Using the financial statement data for Pacific Sunwear, calculate and interpret the company's internal and sustainable growth rate. Using the percentage of sales approach, construct a pro forma income statement assuming a projected growth rate in sales of 19.8 percent.

Pacific Sunwear of California
Detailed Annual Income Statement
(Thousands of U.S. Dollars)

Internal Growth Rate:

Sustainable Growth Rate:

	12 Months Ending 02/01/03	12 Months Ending 02/01/04
Total Revenue	846,393	
Cost of Sales	562,710	
Sell./Gen./Admin.	202,445	
Total Operating Expense	765,155	
Interest, Net	-594	
Net Income Before Taxes	80,644	
Provision for Income Taxes	30,967	
Net Income After Taxes	49,677	
Dividend Yield	0%	

Pacific Sunwear of California
Detailed Annual Balance Sheet (Thousands $)

	As of 02/01/03	As of 02/01/04
ASSETS		
Total Current Assets	182,633	
Land	12,156	
Buildings	26,680	
Leasehold	111,431	
Furniture	148,377	
Depreciation	-97,131	
Goodwill, Net	6,492	
Deposits/Other	9,105	
Total Assets	399,743	
LIABILITIES & SHAREHOLDER EQUITY		
Notes Payable	829	
Accounts Payable	28,456	
Accrued Liabs.	34,522	
Cur.Port.LT Debt	1,521	
Income Taxes	8,000	
Total Current Liabilities	73,328	
Long Term Debt	1,102	
Capital Leases	2,236	
Deferred Taxes	3,015	
Deferred Comp.	7,097	
Deferred Rent	10,574	
Total Liabilities	97,352	
Common Stock	495	
Paid in Capital	93,008	
Retained Earning	208,888	
Total Equity	302,391	

Using the judgmental approach, construct a pro forma balance sheet for Pacific Sunwear using the template provided above. How much external funding will be required to meet the company's projected growth rate of 19.8 percent? What, in your opinion, is the most advantageous form of financing? Why?

PART III

CHAPTER 5
TVM: LUMP SUM CASH FLOWS

Learning Objectives

After reading this chapter, you should be able to answer the following questions.

1. What is meant by the term time value of money?
2. What is the future value of an investment? What is the future value formula? What affect does increasing the interest rate or time period have on the future value of an investment?
3. What is meant by the term compounding? How would the frequency in which money is compounded affect the future value of an investment?
4. What is the difference between simple interest and compound interest?
5. What is the present value of an investment? What is the present value formula? How are present value and future value related?

A fundamental building block of finance is the concept of time value of money. Time value concepts (Chapters 5 and 6) underlie virtually every topic in financial management, including capital budgeting (Chapters 7 through 9). Therefore, an understanding of these topics is vital to the study of the remaining topics in this textbook.

Time value of money is the process of calculating the value of an investment yesterday, today, and tomorrow. It is based on the premise that the original principal will increase in value over time as a result of interest earned. This means that a dollar in hand today is worth more than a dollar promised at some point in the future. For instance, assume that you are offered either $1,000 today or $1,000 one year from today. Are the two offers equivalent? No, because you have the ability to invest the money today and earn interest on it. What if you were offered $1,000 today or $1,250 one year from today? Which offer is preferable? Clearly, it depends on the amount you can earn over the next twelve months. Evaluating these types of alternatives is the essence of time value of money.

There are four basic components to the time value of money: present value (PV), interest rate (I%), compounding period (N), and future value (FV). Each component can be calculated mathematically or using a financial calculator. Both approaches are outlined below.

5.1 Future Value (FV)

The term future value refers to the cash value of an investment at some point in the future. For instance, if an investor were to invest $1,000 in an account that pays 10 percent interest per year, she would have $1,100 in one year. The $1,100 is equal to the original investment of $1,000 plus $100 ($1,000 x .10) in interest. The equation used to calculate future value is:

Equation 5.1
$$FV = PV(1 + I\%)^N$$

Substituting the information provided above, the future value of $1,000 invested for 1 year at 10 percent is in fact $1,100.

$$FV = \$1,000 \,(1.10)^1$$
$$= \$1,100$$

What would happen if the funds were invested for 3 years? The investor would earn the same $100 in interest in the first year but $110 in the second year and $121 in the third year. Do you know why she would earn more interest in years 2 and 3? The reason is that she would earn interest not only on the original investment of $1,000, but also on the interest generated in prior periods. This process of accumulating interest on interest earned in prior periods is known as compounding. By contrast, simple interest pays interest only on the original amount invested.

Going back to the formula, the future value of the investment is $1,331.

$FV = PV (1 + I\%)^N$
$FV = \$1,000 (1.10)^3$
$\quad = \$1,331$

Future value problems can also be solved using a financial calculator. The keystrokes on the calculator are very straightforward. On the HP-10B, which is integrated throughout this text, it would be:

$1,000 PV
3 N
10 I%
FV = $1,331

Let's consider another example. Suppose that $5,000 is deposited today in an account paying 12%. How much will the investor have in 7 years using simple interest? How much will she have using compound interest?

Equation 5.2
Simple Interest = Present Value x Interest x Number of Periods

Accounts paying simple interest provide interest on the original investment only; see *Equation 5.2*. Thus, the investment would grow to $9,200 over seven years assuming a simple interest rate of 12 percent [$5,000 + (($5,000 x .12) x 7)]. By contrast, the investment would grow to $11,053 if the account paid interest that was compounded annually. The difference between the amount earned with compound interest (interest earned on original principal and prior year's interest) and simple interest (interest earned on original principal only) is significant. In this case, the difference is $1,853.41 ($11,053.41 - $9,200) on an investment of $5,000.

Compound Interest:

$$FV = PV(1 + I\%)^N$$
$$FV = \$5,000(1.12)^7$$
$$= \$11,053.41$$

or

$5,000 +/-   PV
7   ■N
12   I%
FV = $11,053.41

In some cases, interest will be compounded more than once per year (e.g., daily, weekly, monthly, or quarterly). In that case, the future value formula must be modified. Specifically, the compounding period, m, must be multiplied by N and divided into I% as follows:

Equation 5.3

$$FV = PV\left(1 + \frac{I\%}{m}\right)^{N*m}$$

Let's assume that the saving account in the previous example compounds interest on a quarterly basis. If so, the future value would be $11,439.64.

$$FV = \$5,000\left(1 + \frac{.12}{4}\right)^{7*4} = \$11,439.64$$

The settings on a financial calculator would also need to be changed to reflect the compounding period. For the HP 10-B, the compounding period would be set to 4 payments per year (4 P/YR) and then the problem would be solved using the same keystrokes.

4 P/YR
$5,000 +/-   PV
7   ■N
12   I%
FV = $11,439.64

Note: If you press the yellow key before pressing N each time, the number of periods will be adjusted for the compounding period (N x P/YR).

5.2 Present Value (PV)

Present value represents the amount that must be invested today to reach a particular investment goal. For instance, suppose that you need $25,000 in three years to start a new business. If you can earn 8 percent on your money, how much do you need to invest today to reach your goal?

Figure 5.1 Time Line

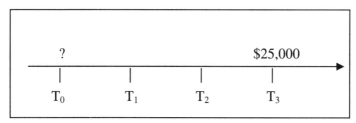

To solve this and other present value problems, the future value formula must be manipulated. Specifically, the symbols should be rearranged to isolate present value.

Equation 5.4
$$PV = \frac{FV}{(1+I\%)^N}$$

Inputting the figures above, the present value would be $19,845.81.

$$PV = \frac{FV}{(1+I\%)^N} = \frac{\$25,000}{(1.08)^3} = \$19,845.81$$

Thus, if you invest $19,845.81 in an account paying 8 percent annually, you will have the funds needed to start your business in three years.

We could also use a financial calculator to solve this type of problem. The calculator keystrokes are provided below.

$25,000 +/-   FV
3   ■N
8   I%
PV = $19,845.81

Literally, every investment goal can be viewed as a present value problem. For example, do you want to be a millionaire? If you are currently 21 years old, and you expect to earn an average of 10 percent each year, how much would you need to invest today in order to accumulate $1 million by the time you reach age 65?

PV = FV [1 / (1 + I%) ^{N}] $1,000,000   FV
PV = $1,000,000 / (1.10) ^{44} or   44   N
    = $15,091.13   10   I%
                                                    PV = $15,091.13

If you invest $15,091 today, the account will grow to $1 million over the next 44 years. Of course, that assumes that inflation and taxes are both 0 percent.

Clearly, though, by looking at these two examples in tandem we can see how powerful compounding can be. Using the same interest rate of 10 percent, $25,000 needed in 3 years has a present value of $18,782.87 while the present value of $1,000,000 with 44 years to accumulate is only $15,091.13. This is the reason that Albert Einstein referred to compounding as "the most powerful force on earth."

5.3 Discount Rate (I%)

The discount rate, denoted as I%, is nothing more than the return on the investment. It is used to compare the performance of two or more investments over time. To calculate the discount rate mathematically, the known variables are inputted into the future value formula. Here is an example.

Consider the following example: Hip Designs CEO, Bob Garvin, invested the $100,000 he received from the sale of his company in 1975. If, in 2001, the original investment had grown to $1,000,000, what rate of return did Bob earn on his investment?

Again, this example illustrates the power of compounding. By investing the sale proceeds in an account earning 9.26% per year, Bob was able to increase his original investment ten fold over the 26 year period.

$FV = PV (1 + I\%)^N$
$\$100{,}000 (1 + I\%)^{26} = \$1{,}000{,}000$
$(1 + I\%)^{26} = \$10$
$1 + I\% = \$10^{1/26}$
$1 + I\% = 1.0926$
$I\% = .0926$ or 9.26%

Preferably, we would solve this problem using a financial calculator as follows:

1 P/YR
$100,000 +/-   PV
$1,000,000   FV
26   ■N
I% = 9.26%

5.4 Compounding Period (N)

The last time value of money concept is the compounding period, or the period of time required to meet your investment goals. Suppose that you deposit $5,000 in an account today paying 10 percent. If you need $10,000, how long will you have to wait? This problem can be solved using three separate methods. The first method involves inputting the known variables into the future value formula as follows:

$FV = PV [(1 + I\%)^N]$
$\$10{,}000 = \$5{,}000 (1.10)^N$
$(1.10)^N = \$2$
$\text{Log}(1.10)^N = \text{Log}(\$2)$
$N = \text{Log}(\$2) / \text{Log}(1.10)$
$N = 7.27$ years

Another method that can be used to determine the compounding period is the Rule of 72. Whenever you are presented with a problem that involves doubling your money this method can be used. The Rule of 72 states that the number of periods needed to double your money is equal to 72 / I%. In this case, 72 divided by 10 percent is equal to 7.2 years. This technique works very well when you are asked to do calculations in your head. For example, suppose that $100,000 is invested in a saving account. How long would it take to amass $400,000 at an assumed rate of 12 percent? Obviously, the investable funds would need to double twice (from $100,000 to $200,000 and from $200,000 to $400,000). Using the Rule of 72, you can quickly estimate that it will take 12 years.

This problem – like all other time value of money problems – can also be solved using a financial calculator. The calculator keystrokes would be:

1 P/YR
$5,000 +/-   PV
$10,000   FV
10   I%
N = 7.27

In aggregate, these four inputs – present value, interest rate, and compounding period, and future value – provide the basis for all time value of money concepts. A basic understanding of these concepts is needed when evaluating different corporate expenditures, determining the most appropriate financing source for the expenditures, and evaluating the effects of the expenditures on the company's present and future value.

END OF CHAPTER PROBLEMS

Questions and Problems
Chapter 5

1. Thanh is offered an investment that requires her to put up $10,000 today in exchange for $60,000 25 years from now. What is the annual rate of return on her investment?

   A. 6.65%
   B. 7.43%
   C. 9.67%
   D. 11.33%
   E. 13.59%

2. Chris has deposited $20,000 in a savings account at Citizens Bank. If the bank offers 12 percent per year compounded daily, how much will his investment be worth in 10 years?

   A. $62,116.96
   B. $66,007.74
   C. $66,389.24
   D. $69,004.23

3. Simin needs to amass $20,000 in five years to begin a business. If she invests $10,000 today, what interest rate will be required to meet her goal?

   A. 12.86%
   B. 13.86%
   C. 14.86%
   D. 15.86%

4. An investment promises to pay 12 percent compounded monthly. If you invest $5,000 today, what will the account balance be in 10 years?

   A. $15,529
   B. $15,872
   C. $16,036
   D. $16,502
   E. $17,126

5. If you invest $1,000 in 2003, how long will it take for the money to double at an interest rate of 8 percent?

   A. 7 years
   B. 8 years
   C. 9 years
   D. 10 years
   E. It can not be determined

6. The process of accumulating interest on interest earned in prior periods is referred to as:

   A. Compounding
   B. Discounting
   C. Annual interest
   D. Holding period interest
   E. Free interest

7. The compounding factor is calculated as:

    A. $(1 + I\%)^N$
    B. $(1 \times I\%)^N$
    C. $1 + I\% - N$
    D. $1 / (1 + I\%)^N$
    E. None of the above

8. Account A provides a return of 10 percent compounded annually. Account B offers a rate of 10 percent compounded daily. How much <u>more</u> money will you have at the end of ten years if you invest $5,000 in Account B?

    A. $0.00
    B. $620.84
    C. $6,020.84
    D. $12,968.71
    E. $13,589.55

9. Your employer is offering to pay you $3,000,000 today or a lump sum of $3,500,000 in 2 years. If the investment rate is currently 5 percent, and it is expected to remain unchanged for the foreseeable future, you should:

    A. Take the $3,500,000 because it has a lower present value
    B. Take the $3,500,000 because it has a higher present value
    C. Take the $3,000,000 because it has a higher future value
    D. Be indifferent, they both represent the same amount of money

10. An account was opened 5 years ago with $1,000, which has grown to $1,400. If the same interest rate was a "simple interest rate" (as opposed to a compounded rate), how much interest would be earned on an annual basis?

    A. $59.60
    B. $69.60
    C. $74.60
    D. $79.60

CHAPTER 6
TVM: MULTIPLE CASH FLOWS

Learning Objectives

After reading this chapter, you should be able to answer the following questions:

1. What is the most efficient method for calculating the future value of multiple cash flows? Can a similar technique be used to calculate the present value of multiple cash flows?
2. What is meant by the term annuity? What is the difference between an ordinary annuity and an annuity due? What is the formula used for calculating the future value of an ordinary annuity? How can the formula be manipulated to calculate the future value of an annuity due? What is the formula for the present value of an ordinary annuity?
3. What is an amortization schedule? Describe the procedure used to amortize a loan into a series of equal payments?

Thus far, we have examined the present value and future value of a single lump sum. In this chapter, we will examine the different methods used to value multiple cash flows. Multiple cash flows involve periodic payments made or received for a given period of time. An understanding of multiple cash flows is critical to the capital budgeting process, which will be addressed in Chapters 7 through 9.

6.1 Future Value of Multiple Cash Flows

The future value of a multiple cash flow problem can be solved using the same basic procedures outlined in Chapter 4 for lump sum cash flows. For instance, suppose that you deposit $3,000 today in an account paying

7 percent annually. In one year, you plan to deposit another $3,000. How much will you have in two years? At the end of the first year, you will have $3,210 ($3,000 x 1.07) plus the second $3,000 deposit, for a total of $6,210. You leave the $6,210 on deposit at 7 percent for another year. At the end of the second year, the account is worth ($6,210 x 1.07) $6,644.70. The time line presented in *Figure 6.1* illustrates the process of calculating the future value of the two deposits.

Figure 6.1 Future Value of Multiple Cash Flows (Example 1)

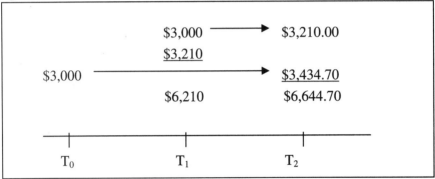

The most efficient method for calculating the future value of multiple cash flows involves first calculating the future value of each cash flow and then summing the results as follows:

$3,000   X 1.07^2 = $3,434.70
$3,000   X 1.07^1 = $3,210.00
                                                       $6,644.70

Let's look at one more example. If you deposit $1,000 in one year, $2,000 in two years, and $3,000 in three years, how much will you have in three years assuming an interest rate of 7 percent? How much will you have in five years if you do not make any additional contributions to the account?

To determine the value in three years, the future value of each cash flow must be calculated individually and then summed as follows:

$1,000 X 1.07^2 = $1,144.90
$2,000 X 1.07^1 = $2,140.00
$3,000 = $3,000.00
$6,284.90

To calculate the future value in five years, the present value of the investment in Year 3 ($6,284.90) will be multiplied by $(1.07)^2$. The result, $7,195.58, is the account balance in Year 5. The problem could also be solved by calculating the future value of each cash flow over five years and then summing the result.

$1,000 X 1.07^4 = $1,310.80
$2,000 X 1.07^3 = $2,450.09
$3,000 X 1.07^2 = $3,434.70
$7,195.59

Figure 6.2 Future Value of Multiple Cash Flows (Example 2)

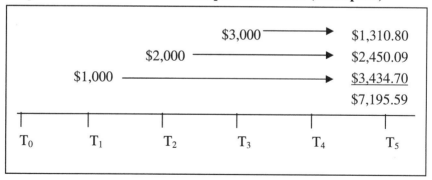

The time line in *Figure 6.2* illustrates the accumulation of each cash flow.

6.2 Present Value of Multiple Cash Flows

Not surprisingly, the same techniques can be applied to solve for the present value of multiple cash flows. For example, suppose you need $2,500 in one year and $5,000 more in two years to satisfy an outstanding debt. If you can earn 9 percent on your money, how much do you have to invest today to exactly cover the future payments?

To solve the problem, the present value of each payment must be calculated. Then, the results are summed to determine the total investment required. In this case, $6,501.98 deposited today will provide the funds needed to meet the debt payments over the next two years.

$$\$5,000 \;/\; 1.09^2 \;=\; \$4,208.40$$
$$\$2,500 \;/\; 1.09^1 \;=\; \underline{\$2,293.58}$$
$$\$6,501.98$$

Financial calculators can be used to solve for the present value or future value of multiple cash flows. For instance, the calculator keystrokes for this problem would be:

1 P/YR
$5,000 +/-   FV
2   ■ N
9   I/YR
PV = $4,208.40

1 P/YR
$2,500 +/-   FV
1   ■ N
9   I/YR
PV = $2,293.58

Figure 6.3 Present Value of Multiple Cash Flows

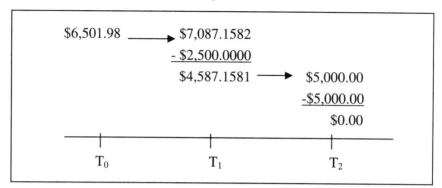

6.3 Annuities

In business, it is not uncommon to encounter multiple cash flows of the same amount. For instance, auto loans and mortgages feature equal payments, usually made at the end of each month. Cash flows that occur at the end of each period for some fixed number of periods are called an ordinary annuity. Alternatively, cash flows that occur at the beginning of each period for some fixed number of periods are called an annuity due. Loans, where payments are made in arrears, are ordinary annuities whereas leases are considered an annuity due since the payments are made at the beginning of the period. The mathematical formulas used to solve annuity problems are presented below.

Present Value of an Annuity (PV_A)

Equation 6.1

$$PV_A = PMT \times \left\{ \frac{1 - [1/(1 + I\%)^N]}{I\%} \right\}$$

Equation 6.2

$PV_{AD} = PV_A (1 + I\%)$

Future Value of an Annuity (FV$_A$)

Equation 6.3

$$FV_A = \frac{(1+I\%)^N - 1}{I\%}$$

Equation 6.4

$FV_{AD} = FV_A (1 + I\%)$

Consider the following example: Suppose you need $25,000 each year for three years to finance the startup costs associated with a new business. The first payment will be made in one year. If you can earn 8 percent, how much do you need to set aside today?

$$PV = \$25,000 \times \left\{ \frac{1 - \left[\frac{1}{(1.08)^3}\right]}{.08} \right\} = \$25,000 \times 2.5771 = \$64,427.50$$

Note: This problem could be solved as a multiple cash flow, but this method is more time consuming.

$$PV = \frac{\$25,000}{(1.08)^1} + \frac{\$25,000}{(1.08)^2} + \frac{\$25,000}{(1.08)^3} = \$64,427.50$$

Financial calculators can also be used to solve annuity problems. In this case, the calculator keystrokes would be:

$25,000 +/-   PMT
3   N
8   I%
PV = $64,427.50

If the payments had started today, we would need to solve the problem as an annuity due. Consistent with mathematical formula, $64,427.50 would be multiplied by 1.08 to arrive at the answer ($69,581.62). To solve the problem using a financial calculator, we would first change the calculator to BEGIN mode and then use the same keystrokes as for an ordinary annuity.

BEGIN
$25,000 +/-   PMT
3   N
8   I%
PV = $69,581.62

Annuity Payment

We can also use the annuity present value formula or financial calculator to solve for the (1) annuity payment, (2) number of payments, and (3) interest rate. For example, suppose you wish to start a new business and need to borrow $100,000. You intend to pay off the loan by making 5 equal annual payments. If the interest rate is 18 percent, what will the payments be?

$100,000 = PMT x [(1 − (1 / 1.18^5)) / .18]
$100,000 = PMT x 3.1272
PMT = $100,000 / 3.1272
PMT = $31,978

Using the present value of an annuity (PV_A) formula, the annual payment can be calculated. In this case, you will need to make five annual payments of $31,978. Of course, the problem can be solved more efficiently using a financial calculator. The keystrokes would be as follows:

$100,000 +/-   PV
5   N
18   I/YR
PMT = $31,978

Annuity Period

Alternatively, you may need to find the compounding period. For instance, suppose that you owe $1,500 on a corporate credit card, and the interest rate is 24 percent compounded monthly. If you make the minimum monthly payment of $50, how long will it take you to pay off the account?

$$\$1,500 = \$50 \times \left[\frac{1 - \frac{1}{(1.02)^N}}{.02}\right]$$

$$\frac{1}{(1.02)^N} = 0.4$$

$$1.02^N = 2.5$$

$$N = \frac{Log(2.5)}{Log(1.02)} = 46.27$$

Whether the mathematical formula or financial calculator is used, the result is the same; it will take 81.27 month (or 6.7 years) to pay off the debt if the minimum payments are made.

```
12 P/YR
$1,500 +/-     PV
$50            PMT
24             I/YR
N = 46.27
```

Annuity Interest Rate

From time to time, you may need to determine the interest rate implicit in an annuity problem. For example, if an insurance company offers to pay you $1,000 per year for 10 years if you will pay $6,710 up front, what rate is implicit in this 10-year annuity?

Unfortunately, this problem is mathematically impossible to solve without trial and error. However, the problem can be solved using a financial calculator. Using a calculator, we see that the insurance company is offering a return of approximately 8 percent.

```
$6,710 +/-     PV
$1,000         PMT
10             N
I% = 8%
```

6.4 Amortization

An amortization table is primarily used to illustrate the payment of debt over time. The table is comprised of five columns: (1) beginning balance, (2) payment amount, (3) interest portion, (4) principal portion, and (5) ending balance. The principal is equal to the payment minus the interest portion. Likewise, the ending balance is the beginning balance minus the principal payment.

Consider the following example: Assume that Urban Outfitters is considering the use of a commercial loan to finance the construction of a new store. Assume further that Citizens Bank has offered the company a $1,000,000, five-year loan at a fixed rate of 8 percent. The loan agreement calls for the company to pay the interest on the loan balance each year and to reduce the loan balance by the amount of principal paid each year. The loan should be fully paid at the end of five years.

The first step in constructing the amortization schedule is to calculate the loan payment using the procedures outlined above. Using the financial calculator, the annual payment would be $250,456.45.

$1,000,000 +/-   PV
5   N
8   I/YR
PMT = $250,456.45

The next step involves dividing the payment into principal and interest portions. The interest component is determined by multiplying the beginning balance each period by the interest rate. For instance, in Year 1, $1 million was multiplied by 8 percent to arrive at the $80,000 interest payment. To arrive at the principal amount, the interest charge is deducted from the payment amount. Now that the annual payment has been divided into principal and interest components, the ending balance is determined by deducting the principal from the beginning balance. Of the $250,456.45 payment made in Year 1, $170,456.45 represents a principal payment. The difference between the $1,000,000 beginning balance and the principal payment of $170,456.45 is the balance remaining at the end of the year ($829,543.55); see *Figure 6.4*.

Figure 6.4 Amortization Schedule

Year	Beginning Balance	Total Payment	Interest Paid	Principal Paid	Ending Balance
1	$1,000,000.00	$250,456.45	$80,000.00	$170,456.45	$829,543.55
2	$829,543.55	$250,456.45	$66,363.48	$184,092.97	$645,450.57
3	$645,450.57	$250,456.45	$51,636.05	$198,820.41	$446,630.17
4	$446,630.17	$250,456.45	$35,730.41	$214,726.04	$231,904.12
5	$231,904.12	$250,456.45	$18,552.33	$231,904.12	$0.00
Total		$1,252,282.27	$252,282.27	$1,000,000.00	

APPENDIX 6.1 TVM AND SECURITY VALUATION

The value of any security – debt or equity – is a function of the future cash flows generated by the instrument. In this section, we will explore how the time value of money concepts introduced in Chapters 5 and 6 can be applied to calculate the theoretical value of various financial instruments.

Valuing Debt Securities

A bond is an interest only loan issued by a company. Investors who purchase these debt instruments receive interest each period until maturity. At maturity, the investor receives the final interest payment plus the original principal that was borrowed. For instance, consider a 10 year bond with a coupon rate of 10 percent and a face value of $1,000. With a coupon rate of 10 percent, the coupon payment would be $100 (0.10 x $1,000). Thus, the investor would receive $100 per year for five years plus the original $1,000 principal in Year 5. To determine the price today (T_0), we would need to discount the cash flows.

Figure A61.1 Calculating Bond Values

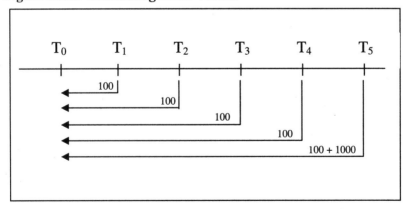

In this way, the value of the bond can be viewed as the present value of an annuity ($100 per year for 5 years) plus the present value of a lump sum ($1,000 received in 5 years). Assuming a market rate of 10 percent, the present value of the lump sum (i.e., principal payment) would be $620.92.

$$PV = \frac{FV}{(1+I\%)^N} = \frac{\$1,000}{(1.10)^5} = \$620.92$$

Likewise, the present value of the coupon payments would be $379.08.

$$PV = PMT \times \left\{ \frac{1 - \left[\frac{1}{(1+I\%)^N}\right]}{I\%} \right\} = \left\{ \frac{1 - \left[\frac{1}{(1.10)^5}\right]}{.10} \right\} = \$379.08$$

By combining the two components, the value of the bond can be determined. In this case, the bond would be valued at $1,000 ($620.92 + $379.08). Therefore, this bond sells exactly for its face value. Is this surprising? No, the interest rate in the market for comparable bonds is 10 percent, which is exactly equal to the coupon payment on the bond.

This problem can also be solved using a financial calculator. The keystrokes are as follows:

$1,000 +/-	FV
10	I/YR
$100	PMT
5	N
PV = $1,000	

Note: The present value of the lump sum and the annuity can be determined in one calculation using a calculator.

When a bond is issued, the interest rate is set equal to the market rate on comparable bonds. However, as time passes, interest rates change in the marketplace. The cash flows on the bond, by contrast, stay the same. As a result, the value of the bond will fluctuate. When interest rates rise, the present value of the bond's remaining cash flows declines, and the bond is worth less (i.e., it will sell at a discount). When interest rates fall, the bond is worth more (i.e., it will sell at a premium). For instance, if the interest rates in the market rose to 13 percent, the value of the bond would fall to $894.48.

$$PV = PMT \times \left\{ \frac{1 - \left[\frac{1}{(1+I\%)^N}\right]}{I\%} \right\} = \left\{ \frac{1 - \left[\frac{1}{(1.13)^5}\right]}{.13} \right\} = \$351.72$$

$$PV = \frac{FV}{(1+I\%)^N} = \frac{\$1,000}{(1.13)^5} = \$542.76$$

Total bond value = $542.76 + $351.72
= $894.48

Again, this problem can be solved using a financial calculator.

$1,000 +/-	FV
13	I/YR
$100	PMT
5	N
PV = $894.48	

The bond now sells for less than its $1,000 face value. Why? The market interest rate is 13 percent. Since the bond pays an interest rate of 10 percent when comparable bonds pay a higher rate, the bond is worth less, and therefore, sells at a discount.

The bond is being discounted by $105.52 ($1,000 - $894.48). Note that the $100 coupon is $30 less than the coupon available on similar investments ($130). In a sense, an investor who buys this bond gives up $30 per year for 5 years. At a rate of 13 percent, this annuity stream is worth $105.52.

13	I/YR
$30	PMT
5	N
PV = $105.52	

What would happen to the price of the bond if interest rates had dropped by 3 percent? Not surprisingly, the bond will sell for more than $1,000. Using the financial calculator, we can see that when similar bonds offer a 7 percent YTM, the bond will be priced to sell for $1,123.01.

$1,000 +/-	FV
7	I/YR
$100 +/-	PMT
5	N
PV = $1,123.01	

The value and status of the bond at various yields to maturity is provided in *Figure A61.2*.

Figure A61.2 Bond Values and Interest Rates

YTM, I%	Bond Value, B_0	Status
7%	$1,123.01	Premium
10%	$1,000.00	Par Value
13%	$894.48	Discount

Valuing Equity Securities

A share of common stock is more difficult to value than a bond because the cash flows (i.e., dividends) are not known in advance. In addition, the life of the investment is indefinite since common stock has no maturity date. Even so, using certain simplifying assumptions, we can determine the present value of the future cash flows (i.e., value) of a share of stock. The current price of a share of stock can be written as the present value of the dividends paid:

$$P_0 = \frac{D_1}{(1+I\%)^1} + \frac{D_2}{(1+I\%)^2} + \frac{D_3}{(1+I\%)^3} + K$$

To value this cash flow stream we need to make an assumption. We can assume that the dividends grow at a rate of 0 percent, or we can assume that the dividends grow at a steady rate, g.

Do any securities provide dividends of a fixed amount? Yes, as a hybrid security, a share of preferred stock pays a fixed dividend (similar to the interest paid on debt). Thus, the dividends on the security grow at a rate of 0 percent. Since the dividend is always the same, a share of preferred stock can be viewed as an ordinary perpetuity with a cash flow equal to the dividends paid.

Equation A61.1

$$P_0 = \left(\frac{D}{I\%}\right)$$

For example, suppose a company has a policy of paying an $8 per share dividend every year. If this policy is expected to continue indefinitely, the stock would be worth $53.33 ($8 / .15) per share assuming a required return (I%) of 15 percent.

Now, suppose that we know that the dividends paid by a certain company are expected to grow at a steady rate. As long as the growth rate, g, is less than the discount rate, I%, the present value of the cash flows can be determined using *Equation A61.2*.

Equation A61.2

$$P_0 = \left[\frac{D_0(1+g)}{(I\% - g)}\right] = \frac{D_1}{(I\% - g)}$$

This equation is referred to as the dividend growth model.

Suppose that a share of stock has just paid a $1 dividend ($D_0$). The dividend is projected to grow at 5 percent per year indefinitely. If the required return is 8 percent, then the price today theoretically should be $35 per share.

$$P_0 = \left[\frac{D_0(1+g)}{(I\% - g)}\right] = \left[\frac{\$1(1.05)}{.08 - .05}\right] = \$35$$

What will the price be in one year? Obviously, it will increase by 5 percent.

$$P_1 = P_0(1 + g)$$
$$= \$35(1.05)$$
$$= \$36.75$$

or

$$P_1 = \left[\frac{\$1.05(1.05)}{.08 - .05}\right] = \$36.75$$

This method would not be appropriate for Urban Outfitters since the company does not pay dividends. Another method that can be used is the price/earnings multiple approach. The price/earnings, or P/E, ratio represents the amount that investors are willing to pay for each dollar of earnings. The price/earnings multiple is a popular technique used to estimate the value a company, particularly those that are not publicly traded. The value is estimated by multiplying the average price/earnings multiple for the industry by the company's earnings per share (EPS) estimate. The industry's price/earnings multiple can be acquired through a number of data providers. Urban Outfitters, for instance, is expected to earn $1.55 per share next year, based on an analysis of the company's earnings trend. The average price/earnings multiple for a company in the retail apparel industry is 26.57. Multiplying the company's expected earnings per share of $1.55 by 26.57 results in a value of $41.18.

To acquire the data needed to calculate the value of a company based on the price/earnings multiple, simply:

1. Launch MultexNet
2. Click the "Fundamentals" tab on the toolbar

3. Enter the ticker symbol for the company in the dialogue box
4. Click the radio button for "All Company Reports"
5. Click "Go"

The quarterly and annual earnings estimates for the next three years are listed in the "earnings estimates" section of the report. To acquire the average price/earnings multiple, the screening tool must be used. The steps are provided below.

1. Click the "Screening Tool tab" on the toolbar
2. In NetScreen Pro, click the "Add/Build" button. Under the Descriptive category, click "Industry Description" and click the "Select" button. The industry box will pop up. In the Industry box, check the radio button for the desired industry (e.g., retail apparel) and then click "Go." You will see the desired industry listed in the criterion box. Click "Go."
3. Click the hyperlink for the number of companies in the industry (e.g., 34). The report provides a list of companies in the industry. In the report, click the "Add/Remove/Arrange Columns" button. Under the Valuation Ratios Category, select the Price to Earnings Ratio (PEExclXorTTM) and then click the ">" button to add the price/earnings multiple to your report.
4. In the report, click "Statistics" and check the radio button for "average." Click "Go" to return to the report. The average price/earnings multiple for the industry will now be listed at the bottom of the report.

If you do not have access to MultexNet, the data can be acquired using Yahoo! Finance. Next year's earnings estimate can be found in the "Analyst Estimates" section. Likewise, the average P/E ratio for the industry is listed in the "Competitors" section.

END OF CHAPTER PROBLEMS

Questions and Problems
Chapter 6

1. At the end of each year for the next ten years you will receive an annuity of $50. The initial investment is $320. What rate of return are you expecting from this investment?

   A. 13.21%
   B. 12.28%
   C. 12.01%
   D. 10.27%
   E. 9.06%

2. You wish to start your own business and estimate that you need $50,000 to cover start-up costs. You have managed to save $35,000 by investing it in a brokerage account with an average annual return of 10.25%. If you make additional contributions of $1,000, how long will it take before you will be able to open your business?

   A. 4.64 years
   B. 3.66 years
   C. 3.49 years
   D. 3.33 years
   E. 2.96 years

Use the following information to answer the next 3 questions.
Cordelia is interested in starting a new business. She has saved $25,000 and needs to borrow another $25,000 to get the business off the ground. Fleet Boston will lend her the remainder at 12 percent compounded monthly for 3 years.

3. How much will Cordelia's monthly payments be?

   A. $830.36
   B. $9,021.64
   C. $9,189.02
   D. $9,403.65
   E. $9,788.48

4. Assuming she pays off the loan over the 3-year period as planned, what will the total cost (principal and interest) be?

   A. $25,000.00
   B. $27,064.93
   C. $29,365.44
   D. $29,892.88
   E. $31,226.17

5. How much interest will Cordelia pay during the first year of the loan?

   A. $766.84
   B. $1,473.60
   C. $2,125.00
   D. $2,603.90
   E. $3,000.00

6. Your broker offers you the opportunity to purchase a bond with coupon payments of $90 per year and a face value of $1,000. If the yield to maturity on similar bonds is 8 percent, this bond should:

   A. Sell for the same price as similar bonds regardless of maturity
   B. Sell at a premium
   C. Sell at a discount
   D. Sell for $1,000
   E. Not enough information to determine

7. Williams Global has a bond issue that has a 5 year remaining life, a $1,000 par value, and a coupon rate of 8% per annum. The bonds are selling to give investors a yield to maturity of 10% per annum. What is the current market price of the bonds?

   A. $1,000.00
   B. $ 959.00
   C. $ 924.18
   D. $ 850.78
   E. $ 796.00

8. Vaidya Corp. has an outstanding bond issue that pays a coupon of 10% per annum on a $1,000 par value, and has 10 years of life remaining. The bonds are currently selling for $887.02 each. What is the yield to maturity on Vaidya bonds?

   A. 10%
   B. 11%
   C. 12%
   D. 13%
   E. 14%

Use the following information to answer the next two questions.

Barr industries will pay a $2.75 per share dividend next year. The company pledges to increase its dividends by 3.5 percent per year, indefinitely.

9. If the required rate of return on the investment is 12%, what is the current value of the stock (P_0)?

   A. $32.35
   B. $33.49
   C. $34.87
   D. $35.69
   E. $36.12

10. If the required rate of return on the investment is 12%, what is a reasonable estimate for the value of the stock one year from now (P_1)?

    A. $33.49
    B. $34.65
    C. $35.69
    D. $36.12
    E. $37.94

CASE ANALYSIS

Loan Amortization
Case 6.1

Assume that Pacific Sunwear is considering the use of a commercial loan to finance the production of a new line of clothing. Assume further that Citizens Bank has offered PSUN a $1,000,000, five year loan at a fixed rate of 8 percent. The loan agreement calls for the borrower to pay the interest on the loan balance each year and to reduce the loan balance by the amount of the principal paid each year. The loan should be fully paid at the end of five years. Using Microsoft Excel, construct an amortization schedule for the loan. Be sure to establish a model (with inputs and outputs).

Loan Amortization

Loan Amount:
Interest Rate:
Loan Term:
Loan Payment:

Amortization Schedule:

Year	Beginning Balance	Total Payment	Interest Paid	Principal Paid	Ending Balance
1					
2					
3					
4					
5					

PART IV

Financial Management: A Practical Guide to Value Creation   171

CHAPTER 7
CAPITAL BUDGETING: DECISION RULES

Learning Objectives

After reading this chapter, you should be able to answer the following questions:

1. What is the net present value? How is it calculated? What is the acceptance criteria?
2. What is the payback period? How is it calculated? What is the acceptance criteria? What are the advantages and disadvantages when compared to net present value?
3. What is the internal rate of return on an investment? How is it determined? What is the acceptance criteria? What are the advantages and disadvantages when compared to net present value?

Capital budgeting is the process of evaluating and selecting a firm's long-term investments consistent with the goal of value creation. The process is comprised of three steps: (1) determining the relevant cash flows for the project, (2) evaluating the merits of the project using one or more investment criteria, and (3) assessing the forecasting risk inherent in the analysis. The various investment criteria will be addressed in this chapter.

7.1 Net Present Value (NPV)

There are four investment criteria that can be used to evaluate the merits of a potential investment: net present value (NPV), internal rate of return (IRR), payback period (PBP), and profitability index (PI). As noted in Chapter 1, the goal of financial management is to create value for the owners of the company. At a basic level, value is created by identifying investments which provide discounted cash flows that exceed the original cost. The difference between an investment's discounted cash flows (i.e., market value) and its cost is referred to as the net present value of the investment.

Equation 7.1

$$NPV = -C_0 + \sum_{N=1} \frac{CF_N}{(1+I\%)^N}$$

For instance, suppose that Urban Outfitters is considering a new investment opportunity. The company's management will first estimate the future cash flows the investment is expected to produce (see Chapter 8). Then, the company's cost of capital will be used as the discount rate to estimate the present value of those cash flows (see Chapter 9). The NPV will then be calculated as the difference between the present value of the future cash flows and the cost of the investment. If the NPV is positive, then the investment should be adopted; if not, it should be discarded.

Based on a pro forma financial statement developed by the company's financial manager, the project is expected to generate $2,500 in the first two years, $5,000 in the next two, and $10,000 in the last year. The project will cost $15,000 to begin production. Assume that the company uses a 10 percent discount rate to evaluate new projects. Should Urban Outfitters proceed with the project?

$$\text{Present Value} = \frac{\$2{,}500}{(1.10)^1} + \frac{\$2{,}500}{(1.10)^2} + \frac{\$5{,}000}{(1.10)^3} + \frac{\$5{,}000}{(1.10)^4} + \frac{\$10{,}000}{(1.10)^5}$$

$$= \$17{,}719.69$$

The present value of the expected cash flows is $17,719.69, but the cost of getting those cash flows is only $15,000, so the NPV is $2,719.69 ($17,719.69 - $15,000.00). Since the NPV is positive, the company should adopt the project. Put another way, adopting the project would increase the total value of the company by $2,719.69.

$$\text{NPV} = -\$15{,}000 + \frac{\$2{,}500}{(1.10)^1} + \frac{\$2{,}500}{(1.10)^2} + \frac{\$5{,}000}{(1.10)^3} + \frac{\$5{,}000}{(1.10)^4} + \frac{\$10{,}000}{(1.10)^5}$$

$$= \$2{,}719.69$$

We can also solve this problem using the financial calculator. The keystrokes are as follows:

-$15,000	CF_0
$2,500	CF_1
$2,500	CF_2
$5,000	CF_3
$5,000	CF_4
$10,000	CF_5
10	I%
NPV	$2,719.69

7.2 Internal Rate of Return

The most commonly used alternative to NPV is the internal rate of return (IRR). IRR is the discount rate that sets the NPV of an investment equal to zero. In other words, it is a rate of return used to summarize the merits of a proposed investment. If the investment's IRR exceeds the required return (i.e., cost of capital), it is a viable investment; otherwise, it should be rejected.

Unfortunately, the only way to find the IRR mathematically is through trial and error. For example, assuming a rate of 12 percent, the NPV would be $1,635.89.

$$NPV = -\$15,000 + \frac{\$2,500}{(1.12)^1} + \frac{\$2,500}{(1.12)^2} + \frac{\$5,000}{(1.12)^3} + \frac{\$5,000}{(1.12)^4} + \frac{\$10,000}{(1.12)^5}$$
$$= \$1,635.89$$

If we continued this trial and error process, we would increase the discount rate to, say, 16 percent. In this case the NPV would be -$261.05. Thus, the internal rate of return must be somewhere between 12 and 16 percent. This process would be continued until we identify the discount rate that sets the NPV equal to zero.

$$NPV = -\$15,000 + \frac{\$2,500}{(1.16)^1} + \frac{\$2,500}{(1.16)^2} + \frac{\$5,000}{(1.16)^3} + \frac{\$5,000}{(1.16)^4} + \frac{\$10,000}{(1.16)^5}$$
$$= -\$261.05$$

Fortunately, a financial calculator can also be used. The keystrokes are:

-$15,000	CF_0
$2,500	CF_1
$2,500	CF_2
$5,000	CF_3
$5,000	CF_4
$10,000	CF_5
IRR	15.41%

If the IRR exceeds the cost of capital used to finance the investment, it is considered viable. In this case, the IRR of 15.41 percent exceeds the 10 percent cost of capital. So, just as with NPV, IRR indicates that the investment will add value.

IRR provides an effective means of communicating the merits of a project. For instance, stating that a project will provide a return of 15.41 percent is easily understood, even by a layman. Even so, IRR is problematic for two reasons. First, it makes the erroneous assumption that cash flows from the project can be reinvested at the current cost of capital. Second, if the cash flows generated by the project are both positive and negative, multiple IRRs will result. For these reasons, NPV is considered the best approach for evaluating potential investments.

7.3 Payback Period

The payback period is the length of time it takes to recoup the initial investment. Consider the project being considered by Urban Outfitters. The project costs $15,000 and provides cash flows over 5 years ranging from $2,000 to $10,000. What is the payback period?

Year	Cash Flow	Initial Cost Remaining
1	$2,500	$12,500
2	$2,500	$10,000
3	$5,000	$5,000
4	$5,000	$0
5	$10,000	

To calculate the payback period, the cash flow generated each year must be subtracted from the initial cost of $15,000. In this case, the payback period is 4 years. Let's assume, however, that the initial cost remaining at the end of Year 4 is $1,000. If so, the project would payoff sometime between Years 4 and 5. Specifically, the company would need to recover $1,000 in Year 5. Since the projected cash flow for Year 5 is $10,000, it will take 1/10 of the year to recapture the remaining cost. Thus, the payback period would be 4.1 years. The shorter the payback period the better since funds are being freed up for other investments.

Due to the simplicity of the calculation, payback period is a useful tool in evaluating small projects. In addition, the decision rule is biased towards short-term projects that free up cash for other investments. As a result, it is biased toward liquidity. Just as with IRR, however, payback period has two drawbacks. First, it ignores the riskiness of the projects being considered; it is calculated the same way for both riskless and risky projects. Second, there is no discounting so the time value of money is disregarded in the calculation.

7.4 Profitability Index

The availability of capital (i.e., investable funds) affects a company's investment decisions. If a firm has unlimited funds, the capital budgeting decision is straightforward: invest in new projects where the return exceeds the cost. Unfortunately, companies do not have an endless supply of capital. As a result, numerous investments compete for available capital. The process of allocating budgeted funds among competing capital expenditures is known as capital rationing. This process is comprised of two phases. In the first phase, capital expenditures are evaluated to determine if they meet the company's acceptance criterion. Those projects that meet the acceptance criterion (including the "best" of any mutually exclusive projects) are then ranked on the basis of a predetermined measure. For instance, all projects could be ranked in descending order based on the internal rate of return as illustrated in *Figure 7.1*.

Figure 7.1 Project Rankings

Project	IRR
D	15%
A	12%
B	9%
C	8%%

As noted above, however, internal rate of return is problematic when evaluating projects with unconventional (i.e., positive and negative) cash flows. To overcome this problem, many companies use the Profitability Index (PI), otherwise known as the benefit/cost ratio. The PI is computed using the same inputs as NPV, but the present value of the future cash flows is divided by the cost of the investment. Urban Outfitter's project costs $15,000 and has a present value of future cash flows of $17,719.69. As a result, the PI would be 1.18. A project with a PI greater than 1.00 indicates that the project adds value to the owner(s) of the company. In this case, the value of 1.18 indicates that for every $1 invested, the company will receive $1.18 in return.

Equation 7.2

$$PI = \frac{\sum_{t=1}^{} \frac{CF_t}{(1+k)^t}}{I_0}$$

Given the fact that NPV and the profitability index use the same inputs, both will provide the same decision (i.e., either accept or reject). However, the profitability index provides a "bang for your buck" measure that can be used in evaluating investments of different sizes. For instance, if Project A has a NPV of $2,000 and Project B has a NPV of $4,000, you would assume that Project B is preferable. But, what if Project A costs $20,000 and Project B costs $200,000? Would you still adopt B if the two were mutually exclusive? The answer would depend on the PI. If used properly, the profitability index allows financial managers to identify the combination of projects with the highest benefit/cost ratio. In doing so, management will maximize the return on budgeted funds, thereby creating value for the owner(s) of the company.

END OF CHAPTER PROBLEMS

Questions and Problems
Chapter 7

1. Barr Industries has identified an investment project with the following cash flows. If the discount rate is 10 percent, what is the present value of the cash flows from the project?

Year	Cash Flow
1	$800
2	$500
3	$1,800
4	$1,300

   A. $2,830.78
   B. $3,100.00
   C. $3,380.78
   D. $4,400.00

2. Which of the following is a correct statement?

   A. The internal rate of return (IRR) is considered to be the most important project analysis technique.
   B. Payback analysis requires the use of a discount rate.
   C. Payback analysis is preferable to net present value (NPV).
   D. If the project has a profitability index greater than one the project is "acceptable."
   E. If the cost of capital is greater than the IRR, the project should be accepted.

Use the following cash flows for a new investment to answer the next three questions.

	Year 0	Year 1	Year 2	Year 3
	-$20,000	$10,000	$10,000	$10,000

3. What is the payback period?

   A. 1.0 year
   B. 1.5 years
   C. 2.0 years
   D. 2.5 years
   E. 3.0 years

4. Given a required return of 25 percent, what is the project's net present value?

   A. -$960.00
   B. -$480.00
   C. $0.00
   D. $480.00
   E. $960.00

5. What is the internal rate for return for the project?

   A. 23 percent
   B. 24 percent
   C. 25 percent
   D. 26 percent
   E. 27 percent

6. Which of the capital budgeting techniques allow a financial manager to rank potential capital expenditures in order to determine which one provides the biggest "bang for the buck."

   A. Net present value
   B. Internal rate of return
   C. Payback period
   D. Profitability index
   E. None of the above

Use the following information to answer the next 4 questions.

Amanda, a pediatric doctor, plans to open an office on Main Street in Waltham. The equipment needed for the office will cost $160,000, and she expects the practice to generate after-tax cash inflows of $40,000 annually over the next 7 years. At the end of the 7 year period, the property is assumed to be worthless.

7. What is the net present value of the project assuming a cost of capital (i.e., discount rate) of 10 percent?

   A. $14,953
   B. $24,658
   C. $34,737
   D. $44,194
   E. $54,039

8. What is the project's internal rate of return? Assuming a cost of capital of 17 percent, should the project be accepted?

   A. 14.1%; yes
   B. 15.2%; yes
   C. 15.2%; no
   D. 16.3%; yes
   E. 16.3%; no

9. What is the project's payback period?

   A. 1 year
   B. 2 years
   C. 3 years
   D. 4 years
   E. 5 years

10. What is the profitability index for this project assuming a cost of capital (i.e., discount rate) of 15 percent? Should the project be accepted?

    A. 0.96; yes
    B. 0.96; no
    C. 1.04; yes
    D. 1.04; no
    E. 1.12; yes

CHAPTER 8
CAPITAL BUDGETING:
CASH FLOW PROJECTIONS

Learning Objectives

After reading this chapter, you should be able to answer the following questions:

1. Define each of the following terms: (1) independent versus mutually exclusive projects, (2) unlimited funds versus capital rationing, and (3) conventional versus unconventional cash flow patterns.
2. Define each of the following costs: (1) sunk costs, (2) opportunity costs, and (3) financing costs. How do these costs affect a project's incremental cash flows?
3. Describe each of the following inputs to the initial investment, and explain how initial investment is calculated: (1) cost of a new asset, (2) installation costs, (3) proceeds from the sale of an old asset, (4) tax on the sale of an old asset, and (5) change in net working capital.
4. What the calculation for operating cash flows? How does depreciation enter into the calculation? What is the difference between straight-line depreciation and the modified accelerated cost recovery system (MACRS)? How does the choice of depreciation method affect the operating cash flows?
5. What is the terminal cash flow? How is it calculated?

As noted in Chapter 7, the capital budgeting process is comprised of three steps: (1) determining the relevant cash flows for the project, (2) evaluating the merits of the project using one or more investment criteria, and (3) assessing the forecasting risk inherent in the analysis. In order to apply the decision rules outlined in Chapter 7, we must first determine the cash flows for the investment in question.

8.1 Cash Flow Patterns

There are two types of projects that are evaluated as part of the capital budgeting process. Independent projects are those projects that are not related to one another; in other words, accepting one project does not eliminate the acceptance of another. Mutually exclusive projects, by contrast, compete with one another. The acceptance of one eliminates consideration of all other similar projects. For instance, a fabric manufacturer that needs to increase production capacity could (1) expand the existing plant, (2) acquire another manufacturer with the needed property, plant, and equipment, or (3) contract with another company that has the needed production capacity.

Regardless of the type of project under consideration, the cash flow pattern will be categorized as either conventional or unconventional. Conventional cash flow projects require an initial cash outflow, which is followed by a series of cash inflows. For example, Urban Outfitters might spend $16,000 today with the expectation of receiving $4,000 per year for the next six years; see *Figure 8.1*.

Figure 8.1 Conventional Cash Flow Patterns

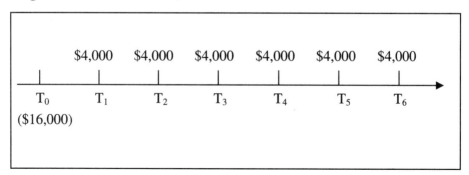

By contrast, unconventional cash flow patterns require an initial cash outflow, which is followed by a series of cash inflows and outflows. For instance, the purchase of a piece of machinery used in the production process might require an initial outflow of $16,000, which is expected to generate cash inflows of $4,000 per year for the next six years. However, equipment may need to be serviced in Year 4 to provide the necessary cash flows for the three remaining years. The cost of service ($8,000) must be netted against the cash inflow of $4,000 to determine the relevant cash flow for Year 4 as illustrated in *Figure 8.2*.

Figure 8.2 Nonconventional Cash Flow Patterns

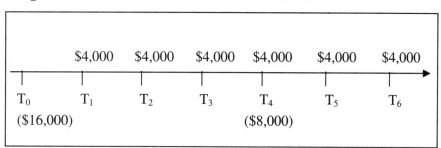

8.2 Incremental Cash Flows

To evaluate a proposed investment, we must consider how the project will affect the cash flows of the firm (i.e., will it add value to the firm?). To do so, we must first distinguish relevant from nonrelevant cash flows. Relevant cash flows, sometimes referred to as incremental cash flows, consist of any and all changes in the firm's future cash flows that result from adopting a project. By identifying the relevant cash flows, the proposed project can be evaluated purely on its own merits.

In order to determine the relevant cash flows for a project, we must first eliminate those cash flows that exist regardless of whether or not we undertake the project. These non-relevant cash flows include sunk costs and financing costs.

1. Sunk costs are those costs that have already been paid or costs that the company has incurred the liability to pay. These costs cannot be altered by our decision to accept or reject the project. For instance, the fee paid to a consultant retained to evaluate projects under consideration would be considered a sunk cost. Regardless of which project is ultimately adopted, the fee must be paid.

2. In analyzing a proposed investment, interest expense, dividends paid, and other financing costs are not considered since relevant cash flows are restricted to those generated by the assets of the project.

In addition to those costs and benefits accruing as a direct result of the project, the relevant cash flows must include the cost of erosion and any opportunity costs. Erosion occurs when a new project cannibalizes the cash flows being generated by a company's existing projects. For instance, if Urban Outfitters introduces a new line of clothing, some of the sales might come at the expense of other lines. If erosion is expected, the cash flows from the new line should be adjusted downward to reflect loss in profits on the other lines. An opportunity cost requires the company to forfeit a benefit. The cost typically arises when the firm owns some of the assets needed for the proposed project. Thus, opportunity cost is the most valuable alternative that is given up if a particular investment is undertaken.

8.3 Project Cash Flows

The incremental cash flows for any investment – whether expansion (i.e., growth) or replacement (i.e., maintenance) – include three basic components: (1) initial investment, (2) operating cash flows, and (3) terminal cash flow. Each component is described in detail below based on a proposed investment under consideration at Urban Outfitters. The company is considering the introduction of a new line of skin care products (i.e., an expansion project), which would be sold through the catalog and retail stores.

Equation 8.1
Project Cash Flows = Initial Investment + Operating Cash Flow
                    + Terminal Cash Flow

8.4 Initial Investment

The term initial investment is used to describe the relevant cash outflows associated with a proposed capital expenditure. The initial investment is assumed to occur today, at time period zero (T_0). For a replacement project, initial investment is calculated based on three inputs: (1) installed cost of the new asset, (2) after-tax proceeds from the sale of the old asset, and (3) any change in net working capital; see *Equation 8.2*. For an expansion project, the initial investment would equal the installed cost of the asset plus any applicable changes in net working capital.

Equation 8.2
Initial Investment = Installed Cost of a New Asset
                    - After-tax Proceeds from the Old Asset
                    + Changes in Net Working Capital

Installed Cost of a New Asset

The installed cost of a new asset is determined by adding installation costs to the acquisition costs of the new asset; see *Equation 8.3*. The acquisition cost is the purchase price of the assets needed for the project, while the installation costs represent any additional costs incurred to put the assets into operation. For Urban Outfitters, the purchase price of the assets is $403,000 and the installation costs are $95,000. Thus, the installed cost is estimated to be $498,000 ($403,000 + $95,000).

Equation 8.3
Installed Cost of a New Asset = Acquisition Costs + Installation Costs

After-tax Proceeds from the Sale of Old Assets

For expansion projects, the after-tax proceeds from the sale of old assets can be used to offset the installed cost of the new assets. The after-tax proceeds are difference between the sale proceeds and any applicable taxes related to the sale; see *Equation 8.4*.

Equation 8.4
After-tax Proceeds from the Old Assets = Proceeds from the Sale of Old Asset +/- Taxes on the Sale of Old Asset

The proceeds on the sale of the old asset would include the net cash flows generated on the same, after taking into consideration any removal costs. The proceeds are typically subject to taxation. The applicable tax will depend on three factors: (1) the initial purchase price, (2) the sales price, and (3) the book value of the asset. If the company sells the asset for more than purchase price, the difference between the sale price and initial purchase price would be considered a capital gain for tax purposes. For business entities, capital gains are added to ordinary income and taxed at the marginal tax rate.

If the purchase price is less than the sale price, it must be compared to the book value of the asset. Depreciation is deducted each year from the original purchase price to arrive at the book value, which is reflected on the balance sheet. There are two depreciation conventions: straight line depreciation and the modified accelerated cost recovery system (MACRS). Calculating depreciation using the straight line method is clear-cut: divide the installed value by the asset's useful life. Calculating depreciation using MACRS is somewhat more complicated.

Every asset is assigned to a particular class (e.g., 5-year class). The asset's class establishes its useful life for tax purposes, and depreciation is computed by multiplying the cost of the asset by a particular percentage.

The typical depreciation classes and the associated percentages are set forth in *Figures 8.3* and *8.4*, respectively.

Figure 8.3 MACRS Depreciation Classes

Class	Examples
3-year	Equipment used for research purposes
5-year	Typewriters, computers, copiers, cars, light-duty trucks, and technological equipment
7-year	Office furniture, fixtures, most manufacturing equipment, agricultural structures
10-year	Equipment used in petroleum refining or in the manufacture of food and tobacco products

Nonresidential real property, such as an office building, is depreciated over 31.5 years. Similarly, residential real property, such as an apartment building, is depreciated over 27.5 years. Note, however, that land is not depreciated.

Figure 8.4 MACRS Depreciation Percentages

Year	3-year	5-year	7-year	10-year
1	33.33	20.00	14.29	10.00
2	44.44	32.00	24.49	18.00
3	14.82	19.20	17.49	14.00
4	7.41	11.52	12.49	12.00
5		11.52	8.93	9.00
6		5.76	8.93	8.00
7			8.93	7.00
8			4.45	7.00
9				6.00
10				6.00
11				4.00
Total	100.00	100.00	100.00	100.00

To illustrate how depreciation is calculated under MACRS, we will consider a cash register costing $5,000. Like computers, cash registers are normally classified as 5-year property. The calculation for depreciation of this asset is illustrated in *Figure 8.5*.

Figure 8.5 MACRS Depreciation Calculation

Year	MACRS %	Depreciation	Book Value
1	20.00	$1,000.00	$4,000.00
2	32.00	$1,600.00	$2,400.00
3	19.20	$960.00	$1,440.00
4	11.52	$576.00	$864.00
5	11.52	$576.00	$288.00
6	5.76	$288.00	$0.00
	100.00	$5,000.00	

In calculating depreciation, we apply a set percentage to the cost of the asset. As a result, the book value of the asset can differ significantly from its fair market value. Suppose the company wanted to sell the cash register after 2 years. Based on historical averages, it would be worth $4,000 (i.e., market value). If it were sold for market value, the company would have to pay taxes at the ordinary income tax rate on the difference between the sales price of $4,000 and the book value of $2,400, or $544 as follows:

Tax Liability = [($5,000 - $2,400) x .34]
            = $544

The difference between the sales price and book value represents excess deprecation, which must be recaptured when the asset is ultimately sold. In other words, the company over depreciated the asset by $1,600. As noted in Chapter 2, depreciation reduces taxable income, and therefore, total taxes due. Since the company deducted $1,600 too much in depreciation when calculating taxable income over the past two years, it paid $544 too little in taxes; the government will require that the company pay the taxes due upon the sale of the asset.

In the case of Urban Outfitters, the proposed investment is an expansion project. Therefore, the after-tax sale proceeds from the sale of the old asset would be zero.

Changes in Net Working Capital

Net working capital, as noted in Chapter 3, is the difference between current assets and current liabilities. Capital expenditures often times result in a change in net working capital. For instance, if a company purchases plant, property, or equipment to expand operations, balance sheet items such as accounts receivable, inventory, accounts payable and accruals will increase. When a company expands operations, it will need additional inventory and accounts receivable to support increased sales. Likewise, the company will increase accounts payable and accruals to support increased purchases. The changes in current assets will be netted against the changes in current liabilities; the result is referred to as the change in net working capital. Typically, current assets increase by more than current liabilities. In that case, the change is treated as an initial outflow for capital budgeting purposes. If, on the other hand, the change was negative, it would be treated as an inflow.

For Urban Outfitters, current assets are expected to increase by $151,500 while current liabilities are expected to increase by $102,000. The difference, $49,500, represents the change in net working capital associated with the proposed investment. Thus, the initial investment would be calculated as the sum of the installed cost of the new asset ($498,000) plus the change in net working capital ($49,500), or $547,500. The initial investment is considered a cash outflow.

8.5 Operating Cash Flows

Operating cash flows are the incremental after-tax cash inflows resulting from a project. These cash flows are calculated using inputs from the pro forma income statement; see *Equation 8.5*. Again, the purpose is to isolate the cash flows of the project. Since depreciation is a noncash expense deducted when calculating EBIT, it is added back. The benefits from the proposed expenditure must be reflected on an after-tax basis. For this reason, taxes are deducted to arrive at the operating cash flow for the project.

Equation 8.5
Operating Cash Flow = EBIT + Depreciation - Taxes
For Urban Outfitters, the proposed project has an expected life of 3 years and the necessary equipment will be depreciated straight-line to zero.

Based on exploratory conversations with potential customers and historical trends in the sales of comparable products, the company projects unit sales of 35,464 (2004), 36,347 (2005), and 37,248 (2006). The new product line will have an average price of $9.99 per unit in 2004. The selling price is projected to increase by 5% per year as the product line gains recognition in the marketplace. Labor costs associated with this project are expected to be $16,500 in 2004. Furthermore, these costs are expected to increase by 3% each year. Similarly, materials costs are expected to be $18,200 in 2003, with annual increases of 7%. Overhead costs and selling, general and administrative expenses are expected to remain fixed at $50,000 and $25,000, respectively. The relevant tax rate is assumed to be 35 percent.

Given these estimates, a pro forma financial statement can be constructed; see *Figure 8.6*.

Figure 8.6 Pro Forma Income Statement

	2004	2005	2006
Price	$9.99	$10.49	$11.01
Units Sold	$35,464.00	$36,347.00	$37,248.00
Revenue	$354,285.36	$381,261.86	$410,248.54
COGS			
Cost of Labor	$16,500.00	$16,995.00	$17,504.85
Cost of Materials	$18,200.00	$19,474.00	$20,837.18
Overhead Costs	$50,000.00	$50,000.00	$50,000.00
SG&A Costs	$25,000.00	$25,000.00	$25,000.00
Depreciation	$166,000.00	$166,000.00	$166,000.00
EBIT	$78,585.36	$103,792.86	$130,906.51
Interest	$0.00	$0.00	$0.00
EBT	$78,585.36	$103,792.86	$130,906.51
Taxes	$27,504.88	$36,327.50	$45,817.28
Net Income	$51,080.48	$67,465.36	$85,089.23

Given the pro forma income statement, the operating cash flow for 2004, 2005, and 2006 can be calculated; see *Figure 8.7*.

Figure 8.7 Operating Cash Flow

	2004	2005	2006
EBIT	$78,585.36	$103,792.86	$130,906.51
Depreciation	$166,000.00	$166,000.00	$166,000.00
Taxes	$27,504.88	$36,327.50	$45,817.28
Operating Cash Flow	$217,080.48	$233,465.36	$251,089.23

8.6 Terminal Cash Flow

The terminal cash flow is the after-tax nonoperating cash flow occurring in the final year of the project. It is the cash flow attributable to the salvage value of the equipment and other assets used for the project, net of any removal costs. For replacement projects, the terminal cash flow would be comprised of the after-tax proceeds from the sale of the new and old asset as well as any change in net working capital; see *Equation 8.6*. For expansion projects, on the other hand, the after-tax proceeds from the sale of the old asset would be ignored.

Equation 8.6

Terminal Cash Flow = After-tax Proceeds from Sale of New Asset
 - After-tax Proceeds from Sale of Old Asset
 +/- Changes in Net Working Capital

The after-tax proceeds on the sale of new and old assets are calculated using the same method employed in the initial investment calculation. If the sale proceeds surpass the book value, a tax payment will be deducted from the sale proceeds to arrive at the after-tax proceeds. If, by contrast, the book value exceeds the sale proceeds, the tax rebate will be added to the proceeds from the sale.

In calculating the initial investment, we accounted for the expected changes in net working capital. With the termination of the project, the increased net working capital needs are expected to end. Since the net working capital investment is not consumed, the amount recovered at termination will exactly equal the amount used in determining the initial investment. For instance, Urban Outfitters estimated a $49,500 change in net working capital. This same $49,500 will be considered a cash inflow in the final year of the project. Since the assets are assumed to be depreciated to zero with no salvage value, the after-tax proceeds from the sale of the new asset will be zero. The cash flow components associated with the project are illustrated in *Figure 8.8*.

Figure 8.8 Cash Flow Components

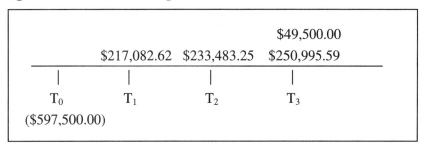

The fixed assets purchased by Urban Outfitters were assumed to be worthless at the end of the third year. However, let's assume that the property purchased by the company will have a $40,000 salvage value at the end of the project. Would the decision to accept or reject the project change? Intuitively, we would expect the cash flow for Year 3 to increase, which will increase the present value of future cash flows and the net present value of the project. The after-tax salvage value is $26,000.

Salvage Value = [$40,000 (1 - .35)]
            = $26,000

Figure 8.9 Cash Flow Components (including Terminal Value)

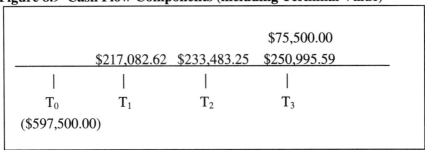

The after-tax salvage value of $26,000 is added to the $49,500 change in net working capital. The result, $75,500, is the terminal cash flow associated with the project.

Figure 8.10 Terminal Cash Flow

After-tax Proceeds from Sale of Proposed Equipment	
Proceeds from Sale of Proposed Equipment	$40,000
Tax on Sale of Proposed Equipment	$14,000
	$26,000
After-tax Proceeds from Sale of Present Equipment	
Proceeds from Sale of Present Equipment	$0
Tax on Sale of Present Equipment	$0
	$0
Change in Net Working Capital	$49,500
Terminal Cash Flow	$75,500

8.7 Investment Criteria

Now that we have the cash flow projections, we are ready to apply the various criteria discussed in Chapter 7, beginning with net present value. The assumed discount rate, or cost of capital, used to evaluate the merits of the project is assumed to be 12 percent.

NPV = -$547,500 + ($217,080.48/1.12) + ($233,465.36/1.12^2)
       + ($326,589.23/1.12^3)
     = $64,898.78

Based on these projections, the project creates $64,898.78 in value and should be accepted. The problem could also be solved using a financial calculator. The keystrokes are as follows:

CF$_0$	=	$547,500 +/-
CF$_1$	=	$217,080.48
CF$_2$	=	$233,465.36
CF$_3$	=	$326,589.23
I/YR	=	12%
NPV	=	$64,898.78

The return on investment obviously exceeds 12 percent (since the NPV is positive at 12 percent). Using the financial calculator, the IRR for the project can be calculated. In this case, it is 18.31%.

CF$_0$	=	$547,500 +/-
CF$_1$	=	$217,080.48
CF$_2$	=	$233,465.36
CF$_3$	=	$326,589.23
I/YR	=	18.31%

In addition, the payback period is 2.30 years.

Year	Cash Flow	Remaining Investment
1	$217,080.48	$330,419.52
2	$233,465.36	$96,954.16
3	$326,589.23	

Payback = 2 + $\dfrac{\$96{,}954.16}{\$326{,}589.23}$

= 2.30 years

8.8 Evaluating NPV Estimates

An investment has a positive net present value if the present value of future cash flows (i.e., market value) exceeds the cost. Positive NPV investments are attractive because they create value for the owner(s) of the company. As noted throughout the chapter, the key inputs in NPV analysis are the projected future cash flows. If these projections are inaccurate, however, the resulting answer can be misleading. The possibility that management makes a bad investment decision because of errors in the projected cash flows is known as forecasting risk. By identifying areas where potential errors exist, we can assess the reasonableness of the estimates used.

Scenario Analysis

The general approach to evaluating cash flows projections involves asking "what-if" questions. There are three forms of what-if analysis: scenario analysis, sensitivity analysis, and simulation. With scenario analysis, we investigate the changes in the NPV estimate that result from asking questions like "What if sales should be projected at 30,000 units instead of 35,000 or what if overhead costs are really $80,000 instead of the projected $50,000?"

Figure 8.11 Scenario Analysis

State	Probability	Present Value of Cash Inflows	Cash Outflow	NPV
Optimistic	0.35	$ 721,335	$ 547,500	$ 173,835
Base	0.45	$ 612,399	$ 547,500	$ 64,899*
Pessimistic	0.30	$ 489,456	$ 547,500	$ (58,044)

* Same facts as assumed above.

The best estimate of project cash flows and NPV is referred to as the base case. To arrive at the most pessimistic (i.e., worst case), we assign the least favorable value to each item. This means low values for items like units sold and price per unit and high values for costs of goods sold and other expenses. The opposite would be true when calculating the most optimistic (i.e., best case) scenario. A scenario analysis for Urban Outfitter's proposed investment is presented in *Figure 8.11*.

Sensitivity Analysis

Another form of what-if analysis is known as sensitivity analysis, which is useful in identifying variables that exhibit high degrees of forecasting risk. By leaving all variables except one constant, we can determine the effects of a change in that one variable (e.g., units sold) on the NPV for the project. If the NPV estimate is very sensitive to relatively small changes in that variable, then the forecasting risk is high. For instance, what would be the effect of reducing the average selling price by $2.00? As illustrated in *Figure 8.12*, reducing the average selling price to $7.99 per unit would result in a net present value of -$53,815. Thus, NPV for this project is very sensitive to small changes in the unit price. In fact, a $2 change in the sale price would alter the decision to pursue the project further.

Figure 8.12 Sensitivity Analysis

Pro Forma Statement	2,004	2,005	2,006
Price	$7.99	$8.39	$8.81
Units Sold	$35,464.00	$36,347.00	$37,248.00
Revenue	$283,357.36	$304,933.16	$328,116.70
COGS			
Cost of Labor	$16,500.00	$16,995.00	$17,504.85
Material Costs	$18,200.00	$19,474.00	$20,837.18
Overhead Costs	$50,000.00	$50,000.00	$50,000.00
SG&A Costs	$25,000.00	$25,000.00	$25,000.00
Depreciation	$166,000.00	$166,000.00	$166,000.00
EBIT	$7,657.36	$27,464.16	$48,774.67
Interest	$0.00	$0.00	$0.00
EBT	$7,657.36	$27,464.16	$48,774.67
Taxes	$2,680.08	$9,612.45	$17,071.13
Net Income	$4,977.28	$17,851.70	$31,703.54

		2,004	2,005	2,006
Cash Flow				
OCF		$170,977	$183,851.70	$197,703
Δ NWC	$ (49,500)			$ 49,500
Cap. Spending	$ (498,000)			$ 26,000
	$ (547,500)	$170,977	$183,851.70	$273,203

Criteria
NPV $ (53,815)   Reject

Figure 8.13 Mutually Exclusive Projects

	Project A	Project B
Initial Investment (Outflow)	$547,000	$475,000
PV of Cash Inflows		
Optimistic	$721,335	$597,231
Most Likely	$615,265	$515,014
Pessimistic	$489,456	$401,854

Decision Trees

Decision trees can also be used to illustrate the various investment alternatives a financial manager may face. A decision tree is a diagram made up of nodes and branches. The nodes denote decision points and the branches represent alternative decisions and their associated probability.

Figure 8.14 Decision Tree

	Initial Investment	Probability	PV of Cash Flow	Weighted PV of Cash flow
Project A	$547,500	35%	$721,335	$252,467
		45%	$615,265	$276,869
		30%	$489,456	$146,837
				$676,173
Project B	$475,000	40%	$597,231	$238,892
		45%	$515,014	$231,756
		15%	$401,854	$60,278
				$530,927

Decision (A or B?)

NPV$_A$ $128,673
NPV$_B$ $55,927

In capital budgeting, a decision tree can be used to determine the weighted present value of cash inflows and the expected net present value for a project. Consider the two projects described in *Figure 8.13*. The present value of future cash flows is based on three different outlooks – optimistic, most likely, and pessimistic – and the associated probabilities. By multiplying the present value of the cash inflows by their respective probabilities, the weighted present value of cash inflows can be determined.

The difference between the initial investment and sum of the weighted present value of cash inflows reflects the net present value of each project; see *Figure 8.14*. In this case, Project A would be preferable since it provides a higher net present value when compared to Project B.

APPENDIX 8.1 USING SIMULATION FOR CAPITAL BUDGETING

Another method used to assess the forecasting risk is simulation. Simulation is an analytical tool used to evaluate the effect of varying inputs on the model output. For example, a financial manager could use a software package such as Crystal Ball to simulate the net present value for a project (i.e., the output), while analyzing the effects of changes in sales price and units sold (i.e., the inputs). When conducting the simulation, a frequency distribution for NPV will be created. From the distribution, the financial manager can determine not only the expected value (i.e., average NPV), but also the probability of meeting or exceeding a given threshold (i.e., level of confidence). Thus, the output of the simulation provides an excellent basis for decision-making because it allows the financial manager to view a continuum of risk-return tradeoffs associated with the project in question.

To understand the use of simulation in capital budgeting, consider the following example:

Urban Outfitters is considering a new capital expenditure. The project has an expected life of 3 years and will require the purchase of $498,000 of equipment to begin production. The equipment will be depreciated straight-line to zero. In addition to the cost of equipment, the project will require an investment of $50,000 in net working capital at the outset. Based on exploratory conversations with potential customers and historical trends in the sales of comparable products, the company projects unit sales of 23,635 (2003), 24,225 (2004), and 24,815 (2005). The new product is expected to sell at $14.99 per unit (with a standard deviation of $1.75). The selling price is projected to increase by 5% per year as Enigma gains recognition in the marketplace.
In a recession, the labor market is expected to be favorable to employers, so wages should not experience large increases. On the other hand,

during times of economic uncertainty, materials costs can display wide swings. Labor costs associated with this project are expected to be $16,500 in 2003. Furthermore, these costs are expected to increase by 2% to 5% each year, with the most likely increase being 3%. Similarly, materials costs are expected to be $18,200 in 2002, with annual increases of 5% to 9%. No single value in that range is more likely to occur than any other. Overhead costs and selling, general and administrative expenses are expected to remain fixed at $50,000 and $25,000, respectively. The expected cost of capital used to evaluate potential projects is 12 percent. The relevant tax rate is 35 percent.

In order to run the simulation, we must identify the assumption and forecast cells. Every Monte Carlo simulation requires that both be assigned before running the simulation. Assigning an assumption means selecting the cell in Excel populated with a simple numerical entry and assigning a relevant probability distribution to it. In this case, we will assume that the sale price is normally distributed with a mean of $14.99 per unit and a standard deviation of $1.75. In addition, labor costs increases are best described with a triangular distribution, while a uniform distribution would best describe materials cost increases.

To apply an assumption using Crystal Ball, simply:

1. Select the cell
2. Click "Cell" and "Define Assumption"
3. From the distribution gallery, choose the appropriate probability distribution (e.g., normal distribution)
4. Enter the information necessary to define the distribution (e.g., mean and standard deviation)
5. Click "OK"

The assumption cells will now be green. As the simulation runs, the computer will pull numbers at random for each of the assumption cells, based on the information you inputted.

Figure A81.1 Assumption Cells

Assumptions	
Sale Price	$9.99
Sales Price Increase	5.00%
Labor Cost Increase	3.00%
Materials Cost Increase	7.00%
Overhead Costs	$ 50,000.00
SG&A Costs	$ 25,000.00
Tax Rate	35.00%
Initial Cost	$ 498,000.00
Useful Life	$ 3.00
NWC Contribution	$ 49,500.00
Discount Rate	12.00%

Assigning a forecast means selecting a cell with a numerical equation and requesting that Crystal Ball capture its output results from the simulation. In this case, the cell containing the formula for NPV will be the forecast statistic.

To apply the forecast:

1. Select the appropriate cell
2. Click "Cell" and "Define Forecast"
3. Enter the name of the cell (e.g., NPV) and the units (e.g., US Dollars)
4. Click "OK"

Figure A81.2 Forecast Cells

Pro Forma Statement		2003	2004	2005
Units Sold		$23,635	$24,225	$24,815
Revenue		$354,289	$381,289	$410,104
Costs of Goods Sold				
Cost of Labor		$16,500	$16,995	$17,505
Cost of Materials		$18,200	$19,474	$20,837
Overhead Costs		$50,000	$50,000	$50,000
SG&A Costs		$25,000	$25,000	$25,000
Depreciation		$166,000	$166,000	$166,000
EBIT		$78,589	$103,820	$130,762
Taxes		$27,506	$36,337	$45,767
Net Income		$51,083	$67,483	$84,996

		2003	2004	2005
Cash Flow Analysis				
Operating Cash Flow	$0	$217,083	$233,483	$250,996
Additions to NWC	-$50,000	$0	$0	$50,000
Capital Spending	-$498,000	$0	$0	$0
	-$548,000	$217,083	$233,483	$300,996

Investment Criteria

Net Present Value $ 46,198 Accept

Before running the simulation, we must set the run preferences as follows:

1. Click "Run" and "Run Preferences"
2. Click the "Trials" button
3. Set the maximum number of trials to 5,000
4. Click the "Sampling" button

5. Uncheck the Random Number Generation radio button
6. Click "OK"

To run the simulation, click "Run" and "Run". The output for the forecast statistic will be captured in the frequency chart throughout the simulation. It can also be viewed on screen by clicking "View" and "Statistics". The results of the simulation can either be exported or included in a report.

To create a report:

1. Click "Run" and "Create Report"
2. Click the radio buttons for the desired output
3. Click "OK"

Figure A81.3 Crystal Ball Report

Summary:
Display Range is from ($125,635.89) to $229,911.91 $
Entire Range is from ($202,595.79) to $299,734.05 $
After 5,000 Trials, the Std. Error of the Mean is $978.95

Statistics:	Value
Trials	5000
Mean	$45,933.22
Median	$45,859.64
Mode	---
Standard Deviation	$69,222.03
Variance	$4,791,688,956.79
Skewness	0.00
Kurtosis	3.07
Coeff. Of Variability	1.51
Range Minimum	($202,595.79)
Range Maximum	$299,734.05
Range Width	$502,329.84
Mean Std. Error	$978.95

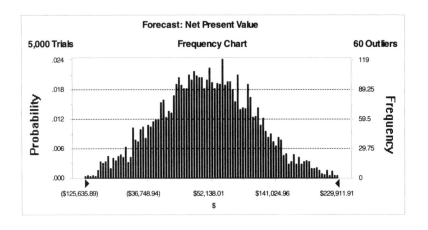

Sale Price

Normal distribution with parameters:
    Mean $14.99
    Standard Dev. $1.75

Selected range is from -Infinity to +Infinity

Labor Cost Increase

Triangular distribution with parameters:
        Minimum   2.00%
        Likeliest   3.00%
        Maximum   5.00%

Selected range is from 2.00% to 5.00%

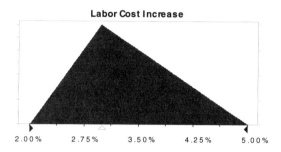

Materials Cost Increase

Uniform distribution with parameters:
        Minimum   5.00%
        Maximum   9.00%

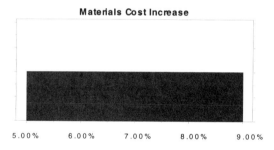

To extract the data:

1. Click "Run" and "Extract Data"
2. Click the radio buttons for the desired output
3. Click "OK"

APPENDIX 8.2 USING SIMULATION FOR CAPITAL RATIONING

Unfortunately, in the real world, a corporation does not have the funds needed to pursue all positive NPV investments. Rather, management must decide which projects to fund, and which ones should remain unfunded. The process of allocating available funds is known as capital rationing. Crystal Ball can be used to extend capital budgeting analysis to include capital rationing. Assume, for instance, that a financial manager at Urban Outfitters is charged with evaluating seven potential capital expenditures.

Using the approach outlined in *Appendix 8.1*, each project was evaluated using Monte Carlo Analysis. The results of 2,000 trials are provided in *Figure A82.1*.

Figure A82.1 NPV Analysis

Statistics	NPV Project 1	NPV Project 2	NPV Project 3
Trials	2000	2000	2000
Mean	$97,882.33	$76,406.24	$83,861.92
Median	$97,853.70	$76,241.81	$83,276.99
Mode	---	---	---
Std. Dev.	$14,217.08	$11,800.23	$17,385.93
Variance	$202,125,478.19	$139,245,331.53	$302,270,619.37
Skewness	0.10	0.14	0.15
Kurtosis	2.96	2.89	3.06
Coeff. of Var.	0.15	0.15	0.21
Range Min	$48,708.32	$41,652.06	$27,115.74
Range Max	$146,850.37	$117,038.95	$147,344.08
Range Width	$98,142.05	$75,386.89	$120,228.34
Mean Std. Error	$317.90	$263.86	$388.76

NPV Project 4	NPV Project 5	NPV Project 6	NPV Project 7
2000	2000	2000	2000
$81,358.44	($6,647.20)	$77,015.71	$73,259.38
$81,426.69	($7,013.16)	$76,276.24	$72,980.86
---	---	---	---
$14,707.02	$14,799.37	$11,794.27	$14,766.62
$216,296,553.32	$219,021,383.92	$139,104,870.44	$218,053,016.06
0.14	0.23	0.23	0.16
3.14	3.25	3.00	3.12
0.18	-2.23	0.15	0.20
$36,020.45	($51,143.23)	$29,326.48	$23,818.18
$135,482.45	$60,551.27	$116,915.89	$135,056.63
$99,462.00	$111,694.50	$87,589.41	$111,238.45
$328.86	$330.92	$263.73	$330.19

With the exception of Project 5, each of the projects has a positive NPV. In fact, the project NPVs range from ($6,647) to $97,882. Thus, six of the seven projects are viable in their own right. If the company were to adopt all six projects, the cost would total $2,286,000. However, the company has budgeted $1,500,000 for projects of this nature. In order to decide how best to allocate the budgeted funds, an optimization model must be constructed.

Monte Carlo simulation requires assumption and forecast cells be identified, whereas optimization incorporates decision variables as well. In this case, the decision is whether or not to invest in each project. Since the projects can either be accepted or rejected, the decision variable is defined as either a zero or a one. Zero indicates that the project is rejected, while a one indicates that the project is accepted.

To identify the decision variables:

1. Select the appropriate cell
2. Click "Cell" and "Define Decision"
3. Enter the name of the cell (e.g., project A) and the upper and lower boundary (e.g., 0 and 1)
4. Click the radio button for a "Discrete Distribution". A discrete distribution means that the decision should must be an integer (i.e., 0 or 1), while a continuous distribution can be a non-integer.
5. Click "OK"

Figure A82.2 Budget-constrained Project Selection

Project	NPV	Cost	Decision
1	$ 95,930.55	$ 376,000.00	0
2	$ 74,881.34	$ 300,000.00	0
3	$ 82,589.28	$ 500,000.00	0
4	$ 78,735.31	$ 400,000.00	0
6	$ 74,881.34	$ 300,000.00	0
7	$ 71,570.63	$ 410,000.00	0
		$2,286,000.00	

Budget	$1,500,000.00
Investment	$ -
Surplus	$1,500,000.00
Total NPV	$ 71,570.63

The forecast statistics will be total investment and the total NPV for the projects chosen. To identify a forecast statistic:

1. Select the appropriate cell
2. Click "Cell" and "Define Forecast"

3. Enter the name of the cell (e.g., Total NPV) and the units (e.g., US Dollars)
4. Click "OK"

To run the optimization:

1. Click CB Tools
2. Click OptQuest
3. Click the New Project icon. This will display the decision variables that were identified in Crystal Ball (i.e., the decision to accept or reject each of the six projects). It will also display the upper and lower bound for each decision variable.
4. Click "OK."
5. The constraints page will be displayed. Click "OK."
6. The forecast page will be displayed. For Net Present Value, click the drop down menu and choose "Maximize". After all, we want to maximize the NPV of the portfolio of capital expenditures.
7. For Investment, click the drop down menu and set the upper bound of the "final value" equal to $1,500,000. This will ensure that the total investment does not exceed the funds available.
8. Click "OK"
9. The optimization will be run until the desired result is found, or until the time limit set runs out. Set the desired number of trials or minutes, and Click "Run"

During the optimization, the best combination of projects will be listed in ascending order in a tabular format. Simultaneously, the performance graph will display the NPV of the portfolio of investments. As the graph creeps up, the computer is closing in on the combination of projects that will maximize the NPV of the portfolio within the established constraints; that is, with the funds available for investment.

At the conclusion of the simulation, the optimal allocation can be reflected in the spreadsheet by clicking "Edit" and choosing the "Copy to Excel" option. To document the results, click "Run" and select "Create Report." The report will include, at a minimum, at overlay chart, which displays the individual net present value of each of the projects being evaluated. This is helpful in determining the individual merits of each capital expenditure. Also provided is the summary statistics for each of the forecasts.

As you can see, $1,476,000 of the budgeted funds was allocated to four investments, which are expected to provide a net present value of $409,494 (mean). The frequency chart displays the range of NPV associated with the combination of the four projects. This chart can be modified to display the probability of reaching a particular goal (e.g., NPV $\geq$ $250,000) by setting the lower boundary at the desired level. Thus, Crystal Ball can extend the analysis to include capital rationing, providing critical information to the financial management that can be used for decision making purposes.

Figure A82.3 Crystal Ball Report

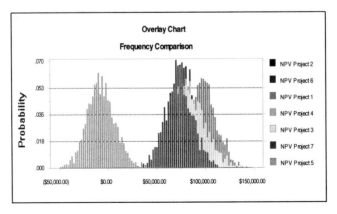

Financial Management: A Practical Guide to Value Creation

Forecast: Investment

Summary:
Display Range is from $1,476,000.00 to $1,476,000.00 Dollars
Entire Range is from $1,476,000.00 to $1,476,000.00 Dollars
After 2,000 Trials, the Std. Error of the Mean is $0.00

Statistics:	Value
Trials	2000
Mean	$1,476,000.00
Median	$1,476,000.00
Mode	$1,476,000.00
Standard Deviation	$0.00
Variance	$0.00
Skewness	0.00
Kurtosis	+Infinity
Coeff. of Variability	0.00
Range Minimum	$1,476,000.00
Range Maximum	$1,476,000.00
Range Width	$0.00
Mean Std. Error	$0.00

Forecast: Total Net Present Value

Summary:
Display Range is from $326,551.51 to $492,436.50 Dollars
Entire Range is from $301,848.03 to $517,939.46 Dollars
After 2,000 Trials, the Std. Error of the Mean is $713.33

Statistics:	Value
Trials	2000
Mean	$409,494.00
Median	$409,168.25
Mode	---
Standard Deviation	$31,900.96
Variance	$1,017,671,137.75
Skewness	0.02
Kurtosis	2.93
Coeff. of Variability	0.08
Range Minimum	$301,848.03
Range Maximum	$517,939.46
Range Width	$216,091.43
Mean Std. Error	$713.33

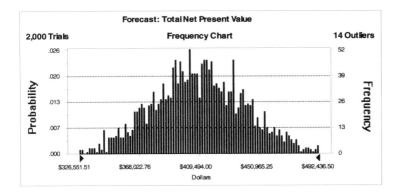

END OF CHAPTER PROBLEMS

Questions and Problems
Chapter 8

1. A company's future cash flows that result from accepting a project are referred to as:

   A. After-tax cash flows
   B. Stand-alone cash flow
   C. Economic cash flows
   D. Incremental cash flows
   E. Fundamental cash flows

2. There are several forms of non-relevant cash flows. _____ are those costs that have already been paid or costs that the company has incurred the liability to pay.

   A. Sunk cost
   B. Erosion cost
   C. Opportunity cost
   D. Bollinger cost
   E. Information cost

3. The risk that errors in forecasted cash flows will lead to poor investment decisions is known as:

   A. Scenario risk
   B. Sensitivity risk
   C. Simulation risk
   D. Forecasting risk
   E. Economic risk

4. The initial investment includes all of the following cash flows except:

   A. Installed cost of the new asset
   B. After-tax proceeds from the sale of the old asset
   C. Changes in net working capital
   D. Operating cash flow
   E. All of the above are included in the calculation of initial investment

5. The calculation of operating cash flow includes all of the following except:

   A. Earnings before interest and taxes
   B. Taxes
   C. Depreciation
   D. Interest
   E. All of the above are included in the calculation of operating cash flow

6. Which of the following is NOT included in the calculation of cash flows from a project?

   A. Capital spending
   B. Operating cash flow
   C. Changes in net working capital
   D. Addition to retained earnings

Financial Management: A Practical Guide to Value Creation   219

Use the following information to answer the next four questions.

XYZ Corporation is considering a new four-year project that requires an initial fixed asset investment of $1.3 million. The fixed asset will be depreciated straight-line to zero over its four-year life. The project will require an initial $25,000 investment in net working capital. The project is estimated to generate $600,000 in annual sales, with costs of $150,000.

7. If the tax rate is 35 percent, what is the pro forma net income for this project?

   A. $600,000
   B. $125,500
   C. $81,250
   D. $43,750
   E. $12,500

8. What is the project's OPERATING cash flow in Year 1?

   A. $0
   B. $81,250
   C. $325,000
   D. $406,250
   E. $600,000

9. What is the project's TOTAL cash flow for Year 4?

   A. $0
   B. $25,000
   C. $406,250
   D. $431,250

10. Assuming a discount rate of 11 percent, what is the project's net present value?

   A. -$1,726,836.34
   B. -$1,325,000.00
   C. -$406,250.00
   D. -$48,163.16
   E. $0

CHAPTER 9
CAPITAL BUDGETING: COST OF CAPITAL

Learning Objectives

After reading this chapter, you should be able to answer the following questions:

1. What is the cost of capital? How is it calculated? What role does it play in making long-term investment decisions?
2. How is the cost of debt calculated?
3. How is the cost of equity calculated? Which approach is preferable for a company that does not pay dividends?
4. How is the cost of preferred stock calculated?
5. What is the weighted marginal cost of capital? How can it be used for planning purposes?

In determining the viability of any project, the relevant cash flows must be estimated, discounted, and compared to the cost of the project. If the discounted cash flows exceed the cost, the project will add value to the owner(s) of the company if it is adopted. But what should we use for the discount rate? As noted in Chapter 2, a company finances its investments through the issuance of either debt or equity capital. Thus, the discount rate used to evaluate potential projects should be the weighted average cost of debt and equity capital used by the firm.

9.1 Cost of Debt Capital

The cost of debt capital is the return that the company's creditors demand on new borrowing. When a company wishes to borrow money, it has two choices; the company can borrow from a commercial bank or it can issue debt securities, which are generically referred to as bonds; see *Appendix 6.1*. If the company plans to acquire a commercial loan, the cost of debt would be the interest rate charged on the new borrowing. If, by contrast, the company plans to use bonds, the cost of debt would be equal to the yield to maturity.

A bond is normally an interest-only loan, meaning that the borrower will pay the interest every period, but none of the principal will be repaid until maturity. With a bond, the coupon is the stated interest payments made on the loan and the face value is the principal amount of the bond that will be repaid at maturity. Bonds generally carry a face (or par) value of $1,000 and have a maturity of up to 30 years. For example, a corporation can borrow $1,000 for 15 years and pay an interest rate of 11 percent. The coupon paid each year will be ($1,000 x 11%) $110. The face value of the bond ($1,000) will be repaid at maturity (Year 15).

Return on Debt Securities

The return on a bond can be described in a number of ways: coupon rate, current yield, and yield to maturity. The coupon rate is the annual coupon expressed as a percentage of the face value. So, a bond with a $125 coupon payment would have a coupon rate of 12.5 percent ($125 / $1,000). By contrast, the current yield is the annual coupon divided by the current price, and the yield to maturity is the rate that sets the price of the bond equal to the present value of its future cash flows.

Urban Outfitters does not have any outstanding long-term debt. However, suppose that the company issued a bond that currently sells for $932.90. Furthermore, assume that the bond pays an annual coupon of $70, matures in 10 years, and has a face value of $1,000. What would be the coupon rate, current yield, and yield to maturity? The coupon rate would be 7 percent, while the current yield and yield to maturity would be 7.5 percent and 8 percent, respectively.

Equation 9.1

Coupon Rate = Annual Coupon / Face Value
= $70 / $1,000
= 7 percent

Equation 9.2

Current Yield = Annual Coupon / Current Price
= $70 / $932.90
= 7.5 percent

The yield to maturity can only be calculated mathematically using trial and error:

Try 10 percent: $70 \times (1 - 1/(1.10)^{10})/.10 + \$1,000(1.10)^{10} = \$816$
Try 8 percent: $\$70 \times (1 - 1/(1.08)^{10})/.10 + \$1,000(1.08)^{10} = \$933$
YTM = ~8%

A financial calculator provides a more efficient method for solving YTM. To do so, set it up as you would any other TVM problem:

$1,000	FV
$932.90 +/-	PV
$70	PMT
10	N
I/YR = 8.0094	

In determining the cost of debt capital, the coupon rate is irrelevant. The coupon rate simply infers the cost of debt when it was originally issued. The current cost of debt, denoted R_D, is the yield to maturity. However, the interest paid on debt is a tax deductible expense (unlike payments to owners, such as dividends). Thus, we need to distinguish between the pretax and after tax cost of debt. The after tax cost can be written as $R_D(1 - T)$, where T is the marginal tax rate for the company. Assuming a tax rate of 35 percent, the after-tax cost of debt would be 5.20 percent [.08 (1 - .35)].

Interest Rates and Bond Values

As noted in *Appendix 6.1*, bond prices and interest rates move in opposite directions. When interest rates rise, bond values decline. Similarly, when interest rates fall, bond values rise. Thus, even when considering a bond that is riskless in the sense that the borrower is certain to make all the payments, there is still risk inherent in owning the bond. The risk that arises from fluctuating interest rates is known as interest rate risk.

The sensitivity of a bond's price to interest rate changes dictates the amount of interest rate risk associated with that bond. The degree of sensitivity depends on two factors: the time to maturity and the coupon rate. Specifically, the longer the time to maturity, the greater the interest rate risk. Likewise, the lower the coupon rate, the greater the interest rate risk. The reason that longer-term bonds have greater interest rate sensitivity is that a large portion of a bond's value stems from the face value. The reason that bonds with lower coupons have greater interest rate risk is essentially the same. By contrast, a bond with a higher coupon generates more cash flow in the early stages of the contract, so its value is less sensitive to changes in the discount rate.

Bond Ratings

The interest rate charged on debt is a function of the company's credit rating. At present, there are two leading bond rating firms: Moody's and Standard and Poor's (S&P). The credit ratings are an assessment of the creditworthiness of the issuing company. Thus, the ratings only concern the possibility of default; they do not address interest rate risk. The highest rating a company can receive is AAA (S&P) or Aaa (Moody's), indicating the company has a low degree of credit risk. The lowest rating is D (S&P) or C (Moody's), reflecting the fact that a company's debt is in default.

Figure 9.1 Bond Ratings

	Standard & Poor's	Moody's
Highest Quality	AAA	Aaa
High Quality	AA	Aa
Upper Medium Quality	A	A
Medium Quality	BBB	Baa
Speculative	BB	Ba
Low Quality	B	B
Low Quality, Default Possible	CCC	Caa
Low Quality, Partial Recovery Possible	CC, C	Ca
Default, Recovery Unlikely	D	C

The term investment grade is used to describe bonds rated BBB (S&P) or Baa (Moody's) or better. Any debt rated below a BBB is considered non-investment grade or "junk". The bond rating for a company can be acquired using a variety of financial technologies, including Bloomberg. To access the bond rating for a publicly traded company in Bloomberg:

1. Type the ticker symbol for the company (e.g., URBN)
2. Press the F8 key (i.e., equity)
3. Type CRPR (i.e.,)
4. Press GO

If you do not have access to Bloomberg, a company's bond rating can be acquired using Yahoo! Finance.

Since Urban Outfitters does not have long-term debt, there is no bond rating for the company.

9.2 Cost of Equity Capital

The cost of equity is the return that equity investors require on their investment in the company. There are two approaches to determining the cost of equity: dividend growth model (DGM) approach and the capital asset pricing model (CAPM) approach.

Return on Equity Securities: Dividend Growth Model Approach

The easiest way to estimate the cost of equity capital is to use the dividend growth model. If we assume that a company's dividends will grow at a constant rate, g, the price per share of stock outstanding, P_0, can be written as:

Equation 9.3

$$P_0 = \frac{D_0(1+g)}{(r-g)} = \frac{D_1}{(r-g)}$$

where D_0 is the dividend just paid, D_1 is the dividend to be paid next period, g is the growth rate in dividends, and r is the required rate of return. The formula can be rearranged to solve for the required return, r (i.e., cost of equity, R_E), as follows:

Equation 9.4

$$R_E = \frac{D_1}{P_0} + g$$

To effectively use the dividend growth model, historical data must be acquired and used to estimate the growth rate in the company's dividends. As noted in Chapter 3, Urban Outfitters does not pay dividends. However, for the purpose of demonstrating the dividend growth model, assume that the company has paid dividends over the past ten years and that the current price is $20.70; see *Figure 9.2*.

Calculating the average growth rate requires (1) calculating the growth rate for each year, (2) summing the rates, and (3) dividing by the number of years. Using the dividend growth model, the cost of equity, R_E, is 11.72 percent.

R_E = [($.0943 x 1.1121) / $20.70] + .1121
  = 11.72%

Figure 9.2 Historical Dividends per Share

Year	DPS	Growth
1993	$0.0326	
1994	$0.0363	11.21%
1995	$0.0403	11.21%
1996	$0.0448	11.21%
1997	$0.0499	11.21%
1998	$0.0555	11.21%
1999	$0.0617	11.21%
2000	$0.0686	11.21%
2001	$0.0763	11.21%
2002	$0.0848	11.21%
2003	$0.0943	11.21%

The principal advantage of using the dividend growth model to calculate the cost of equity capital is simplicity. It can be easily calculated using the historical dividends paid by the company in question. However, there are a number of problems with this approach. First, the model is only applicable to companies that pay dividends. Moreover, the dividends are assumed to grow at a constant rate. To overcome these limitations, many financial managers use the capital asset pricing model described below.

Return on Equity Securities: Capital Asset Pricing Model Approach

The capital asset pricing model (CAPM) provides a benchmark for the required rate of return on an equity security based on its relationship to risk. As such, it can be used to determine the cost of equity as follows:

Equation 9.5

$$R_E = R_f + \beta(R_m - R_f) + e$$

At a basic level, investors have the option of either investing in a risk-free asset (e.g., Treasury bills) or in a risky asset (e.g., equity securities). The risk-free rate of return, R_f, is therefore the return that the investor would receive by investing in T-bills.

Beta, denoted β, is a measure of riskiness of an equity security in relation to the broad market (i.e., S&P 500). The beta of the market is 1.0. If a particular security has a beta of 2.0, the security is twice as risky as the broad market; 0.5 would indicate that it is half as risky. Urban Outfitters, for instance, has a beta of 1.25, indicating that it is 1.25 times as risky as the S&P 500. Beta can be calculated using historical price data for the security and the S&P 500. Specifically, the covariance between the security and the market is divided by the variance of the market; see *Equation 9.6*.

Financial Management: A Practical Guide to Value Creation   229

Equation 9.6

$$\beta = \frac{Cov_{E,M}}{\sigma_M^2}$$

The difference between the return on the market and the return on the risk free rate, denoted ($R_M - R_f$), is known as the risk premium. It is multiplied by the beta coefficient to reflect the risk premium for the security (rather than the broad market) under consideration.

To illustrate, let's calculate the cost of equity for Urban Outfitters. The beta coefficient for the company is 1.25. Assume that the T-bill rate is currently 4.02 percent and the market risk premium is 5.5 percent. Given this data, the company's cost of equity can be calculated. It is 10.9 percent.

$R_E = 4.02\% + 1.25\ (5.50\%)$
$\quad = 10.90\%$

The capital asset pricing model approach has two principal advantages. First, it reflects the risk associated with the company. In addition, it is applicable to companies other than those that pay dividends that grow at a constant rate. The disadvantage is that the model requires an estimation of beta. Therefore, it is only applicable for companies that are publicly traded.

9.3 Cost of Retained Earnings

Net income is used to pay dividends to the company's owners. The payment of dividends reduces retained earnings in any given year. Thus, if management decides to finance a new investment with equity capital, it has two alternatives: it could issue additional equity in the company or it could retain company earnings. If the company retains the necessary funds, the shareholders do not receive cash dividends. As a result, the retention of net income increases equity capital in the same way that the sale of additional shares would. For this reason, the cost of retained earnings is the same as the cost of a comparable issue of equity.

9.4 Cost of New Issues of Common Equity

If sufficient funds are not available through retained earnings, then the company will need to issue new common equity or debt. New equity is underpriced (i.e., sold at a discounted price) and includes transaction costs. Thus, the net proceeds from the sale will always be less than the current market value, P_0, and the cost of new equity (R_{NE}) will always be higher than the cost of existing equity (and therefore retained earnings).

9.5 Cost of Preferred Stock

In addition to common equity, firms use preferred stock to finance their investments. Preferred stock is considered a hybrid security; it has a fixed dividend paid each period. As a result, it can be viewed as a perpetuity. Thus, the cost of preferred stock, R_p, is:

Equation 9.7

$$R_P = \frac{D}{P_0}$$

To better understand the cost of preferred stock consider the following example: On March 12, 2003, a retail apparel company issued preferred stock. The issue pays $6.50 per share per year and currently sells for $81 per share. What is the cost of preferred stock for this company?

R_p = $6.50 / $81
= 8.02%

In this case, the cost of preferred would be 8.02 percent.

9.6 Weighted Average Cost of Capital

To calculate the weighted average cost of capital, you must know the weight and cost of each component. The weight is a function of the market value of each capital component. To determine the market value of the company's equity, denoted E, we must multiply the number of shares outstanding by the price per share. Similarly, the market value of the company's debt, D, is calculated by multiplying the market price of one bond by the number of bonds outstanding. If the debt is not publicly traded, we must observe the yields on similar, publicly traded debt; this is known as the pure play approach.

V can be used to represent the combined market value of the debt and equity capital used by a company.

Equation 9.8
$$V = E + D$$

If the firm also has preferred stock outstanding, V would be expanded to include P (calculated as the product of the price and shares outstanding) as follows:

Equation 9.9
$$V = E + D + P$$

By dividing each component by V, we can arrive at the proportion of debt and equity financing used by the company. These percentages (E/V, D/V, and P/V) are often called the capital structure weights.

For example, if the total market value of a company's equity capital is $500 million and the company's debt is $250 million, then the combined value would be $750 million. Of this total, E/V would represent 67 percent of the firm's financing; the remaining proportion – 33 percent – would represent debt financing.

To calculate the firm's overall cost of capital, the capital structure weights are multiplied by the associated costs and the resulting products are summed. The result is the weighted average cost of capital, or WACC.

Equation 9.10
$$WACC = (E/V)R_E + [(D/V)R_D(1-T)] + (P/V)R_P$$

WACC is the overall return the company must earn on its new investments to retain its current value. Since Urban Outfitters has not issued long-term debt or preferred stock, the company's weighted average cost of capital would be equal to the cost of equity (10.90%).

To better understand the calculation of WACC for a company with a more complex capital structure, consider DPG Oil. The company has an assumed target capital structure of 50 percent common stock, 15 percent preferred stock, and 35 percent long-term debt. The company's cost of equity is 15 percent, the cost of preferred stock is 8 percent, and the cost of long-term debt is 6 percent. With a relevant tax rate is 34 percent, the company's WACC would be 10.09%.

$$WACC = (.50).15 + (.35)[.06(1-.34)] + (.15).08$$
$$= .1009$$

Thus, the cost of capital used as a discount rate in evaluating potential investments would be 10.09 percent.

9.7 Weighted Marginal Cost of Capital

The company's cost of capital is a key ingredient to the capital budgeting process. Specifically, a company should only undertake investments for which the expected return (i.e., IRR) is greater than the weighted average cost of capital. However, a company's cost of capital will change over time with the volume of financing. As the volume increases, the cost of financing increases, thereby increasing the weighted average cost of capital. For this reason, it is helpful to compute the weighted marginal cost of capital; that is, the weighted average cost of capital associated with the next dollar of financing.

When compared to new equity issues, retained earnings provides a less expensive form of equity financing. So, once the retained earnings of the company have been depleted, the weighted average cost of capital will increase with the substitution of the more expensive equity issue. In addition, the company's investors and creditors require a return (e.g., dividends and interest) that is commensurate with the risk being taken. As the amount of financing increases, the risk associated with debt and equity claims also increases. Thus, the weighted marginal cost of capital is an increasing function of the level of total financing.

Calculating the weighted marginal cost of capital is a two-step process. First, we must calculate the break point, or the level at which the cost of one of the financing components increases. The breakpoint formula is provided below.

Equation 9.5

$$BP_i = \frac{F_i}{w_i}$$

In other words, the break point for financing source i, BP_i, is determined by dividing the amount of funds available from a particular financing source (F_i) by the capital structure weight (w_i). For instance, assume that DPG Oil depletes the $250,000 in retained earnings (R_{RE} = 15%). The company would then need to sell new common stock (R_{NE} = 16%) to meet its equity financing needs. Moreover, the company's creditors have indicated that it can borrow $400,000 of debt at 3.96 percent (R_D). Any addition debt will cost 6.5 percent after-tax. Thus, two breakpoints exist – up until the $250,000 in retained earnings is depleted and then at the point where the $400,000 in debt is depleted. Using *Equation 9.5*, the respective breakpoints are:

$$BP_{CS} = \frac{F_{CS}}{w_{CS}} = \frac{\$250,000}{0.50} = \$500,000$$

$$BP_D = \frac{F_D}{w_D} = \frac{\$400,000}{0.35} = \$1,142,857$$

After the break points are determined, the second step is to calculate the weighted average cost of capital between the various breakpoints. Thus, the cost of capital between zero and first breakpoint is calculated, then the first and second breakpoint, and so on. In aggregate, this data can be used to calculate the weighted marginal cost of capital.

The weighted marginal cost of capital for the three financing ranges is summarized in *Figure 9.3*. By comparing the cost of capital in column 4 for each of the three ranges, it should be obvious that the cost from zero to $500,000 is the same as predicted earlier; that is, the current weighted average cost of capital. The second range from $500,000 to $1,142,857 reflects the increase in the cost of equity to 16 percent, and the third reflects the increase in the cost of long-term debt to 6.5 percent. These ranges can be used in evaluating proposed investments by adjusting the cost of capital used in the various evaluation criteria.

Figure 9.3 Weighted Marginal Cost of Capital

Range	Capital	Weight	Cost	Weighted Cost
$0-$500,000	Debt	0.35	3.96%	1.39%
	Preferred Stock	0.15	8.00%	1.20%
	Common Stock	0.50	15.00%	7.50%
				10.09%
$500,000-$1,142,857	Debt	0.35	3.96%	1.39%
	Preferred Stock	0.15	8.00%	1.20%
	Common Stock	0.50	16.00%	8.00%
				10.59%
$1,142,857 +	Debt	0.35	6.50%	2.28%
	Preferred Stock	0.15	8.00%	1.20%
	Common Stock	0.50	16.00%	8.00%
				11.48%

9.8 Other Considerations

Using WACC as the discount rate for future cash flows is only appropriate when the proposed investment is consistent with the company's current line of business; for instance, a retailer such as Urban Outfitters thinking of opening a new store. When evaluating projects with risks that are significantly different, WACC must be adjusted. Otherwise, it will lead to poor investment decisions. In fact, a company that uses WACC to evaluate all projects will accept risky, unprofitable investments. To overcome this problem, a company entering a new line of business can devise an appropriate cost of capital by examining the required returns of companies operating in that industry.

The same situation can arise in a company operating more than one line of business. In that case, the company will need to develop separate divisional costs of capital that can be applied in evaluating potential projects.

END OF CHAPTER PROBLEMS

Questions and Problems
Chapter 9

1. Barr Industries' bonds have a face value of $1,000 and a 10 percent coupon paid semi-annually until maturity 7 years from now. What is the current yield on this issue if the yield to maturity is 7 percent?

   A. 4.62%
   B. 8.59%
   C. 8.83%
   D. 9.04%
   E. 9.25%

2. Owen Oil has an outstanding debt issue that pays a coupon of 10% per year on a $1,000 par value, and has 10 years remaining until maturity. The bonds are currently selling for $887.02 each. What is the yield to maturity on Owen's debt?

   A. 10%
   B. 11%
   C. 12%
   D. 13%
   E. 14%

   Note: This same calculation would be used to determine the company's cost of debt.

3. A company plans to pay a $3.00 per share dividend next period. The company pledges to increase its dividend by 5 percent per year, indefinitely. If the current price of the company's common stock is $21, what is the cost of equity, R_E?

    A. 5.00%
    B. 9.29%
    C. 14.29%
    D. 19.29%
    E. None of the above

4. If the beta for a company is 1.2 and the current T-bill rate is 4.5 percent, what is the company's cost of equity, R_E, assuming a market return of 9 percent?

    A. 9.00%
    B. 9.50%
    C. 9.90%
    D. 10.00%
    E. None of the above

5. Kayhan Electronics has a target capital structure of 60 percent common stock 10 percent preferred stock, and 30 percent debt. Its cost of equity is 15 percent, the cost of preferred stock is 7 percent, and the cost of debt is 8 percent. The relevant tax rate is 34 percent. What is the company's WACC?

    A. 11.28%
    B. 12.10%
    C. 13.4%
    D. 14.6%
    E. None of the above

6. A firm's assets can be financed through debt, common stock, and preferred stock. The proportion of each is known as the firm's:

   A. Standard deviation
   B. Portfolio weight
   C. Cost of capital
   D. Capital structure weight
   E. Beta coefficient

7. A measure of a company's long-term financing costs, which can be used as a benchmark for required return on an investment is referred to as:

   A. Reward to risk ratio
   B. Beta coefficient
   C. Weighted average cost of capital (WACC)
   D. Weighted marginal cost of capital
   E. None of the above

8. A company's cost of debt _____ .

   A. is the return that the firm's creditors demand for new borrowings
   B. can be calculated using the capital asset pricing model
   C. can be estimated by finding the yield on recently-issued bonds with lower bond ratings
   D. is the coupon rate being paid on existing bonds of with a comparable credit rating
   E. None of the above

9. Which of the following is true about WACC?

   A. It requires that the cost of equity be multiplied by (1 – tax rate).
   B. It is an indicator of whether or not the company's equity is overvalued or undervalued.
   C. It is the minimum return that investors require from the company.
   D. It is the minimum return that equity holders require from the company.
   E. Preferred stock is not included in the calculation of WACC.

10. Supposed that Bolton Electronics has a cost of equity of 14% and a cost of debt of 9%. If the target debt/equity ratio is 75%, and the tax rate is 34%, what is Bolton's weighted average cost of capital (WACC)?

    A. 6.6%
    B. 7.9%
    C. 8.4%
    D. 10.5%
    E. 10.9%

PART V

CHAPTER 10
RISK AND RETURN

Learning Objectives

After reading this chapter, you should be able to answer the following questions:

1. What are the measures of return? What are the basic components of the holding period return? What is the difference between average return and geometric return?
2. What are the basic measures of return? What is the difference between systematic and nonsystematic risk? Explain how risk relates to financial decision-making.

The purpose of capital budgeting is to identify investments that will add value to the company. The value added will make the company more attractive to potential investors. However, the value added will be distributed to the company's investors in different ways. Debtholders receive a fixed payoff of principal and interest if the value of the firm is sufficient to cover the obligation. Equityholders, on the other hand, receive a residual claim; they are paid dividends after the principal and interest payments have been made and receive the residual in liquidation after the commitments to all debtholders have been met.

Investors require a return that is commensurate with the risk being borne. Since equity (i.e, common stock) is riskier than debt (i.e., bonds), common stock provides a higher rate of return on average. The historical returns on the various financial claims provide evidence of the positive relationship between risk and return. Specifically, the average annual returns have been lowest for U.S. Treasury bills (i.e., risk-free assets) and highest for volatile, small cap stocks. In fact, from 1926-2003, the average return on T-bills was 3.8 percent per year. During the same period, common stock issued by the 500 largest companies in the U.S. (i.e., members of the S&P 500) generated an average annual return of 12.4 percent; see *Figure 10.1* for more details.

Figure 10.1 Total Returns
Summary Statistics of Annual Returns from 1926 to 2003

Asset Class	Geometric Return	Arithmetic Return	Standard Deviation
Large Company Stocks	10.4%	12.4%	20.4%
Small Company Stocks	12.7%	17.5%	33.3%
Long-term Corporate Bonds	5.9%	6.2%	8.6%
Long-term Government Bonds	5.4%	5.8%	9.4%
Intermediate-term Government Bonds	5.4%	5.5%	5.7%
US Treasury Bills	3.7%	3.8%	3.1%
Inflation	3.0%	3.1%	4.3%

Source: Stocks, Bonds, Bills, and Inflation ® 2004 Yearbook, Ibbotson Associates.

The rate of return on an investment will have a significant impact on the future value of an investment. *Figure 10.2* illustrates the growth of $1.00 invested in the various asset classes from 1926 to 2003.

10.1 Measures of Return

The rate of return on an investment – regardless of the nature of the claim – can be calculated in either percentage or dollar terms. Dollar returns come in two forms: periodic income and capital appreciation. For instance, if 100 shares of stock are purchased at $21 per share and the price appreciates to $22.50, the difference ($1.50 per share) represents a gain on the security. If, on the other hand, the price depreciates to $20.75, the investor would suffer a loss of $0.25 per share, assuming no dividends were paid during the period. Any dividends paid during the period would be added to the price change.

Figure 10.2 Wealth Indices of Investments
Year-end 1925 = $1.00

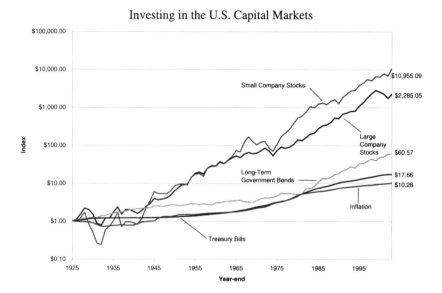

Source: Stocks, Bonds, Bills, and Inflation ® 2004 Yearbook, Ibbotson Associates.

When making investment decisions, it is often more convenient to use percentage returns since they apply regardless of the dollar amount being invested. To convert a dollar return to a percentage return, the sum of income and capital appreciation received during the period are divided by the initial investment. The result is referred to as the holding period return (HPR).

Equation 10.1
$$\text{HPR} = \frac{\text{Ending Value}(P_1) - \text{Beginning Value}(P_0) + \text{Income}}{\text{Beginning Value}(P_0)}$$

For instance, assume that you bought Urban Outfitters on September 26,

2002 for $23. After holding the security for one year, you sold it for $26.25 on September 26, 2003. What is the holding period return? Given the fact that the company does not pay dividends, the holding period return would be equal to capital appreciation during the one year period divided by the original price, or 15.22 percent.

$$\text{Holding Period Return} = \frac{\$26.50 - \$23.00 + \$0.00}{\$23.00} = 15.22\%$$

Figure 10.3 Total Income Returns and Capital Appreciation

Summary Statistics of Annual Returns from 1926 to 2003

Asset Class	Geometric Return	Arithmetic Return	Standard Deviation
Large Company Stocks	10.4%	12.4%	20.4%
Income	4.3%	4.3%	1.5%
Capital Appreciation	5.9%	7.8%	19.7%
Long-term Government Bonds	5.4%	5.8%	9.4%
Income	5.2%	5.2%	2.8%
Capital Appreciation	0.0%	0.3%	8.2%
Intermediate-term Government Bonds	5.4%	5.5%	5.7%
Income	4.7%	4.8%	3.0%
Capital Appreciation	0.5%	0.6%	4.5%
Inflation	3.0%	3.1%	4.3%

Source: Stocks, Bonds, Bills, and Inflation ® 2004 Yearbook, Ibbotson Associates.

When evaluating the return on a security over multiple periods, an investor can use either (1) the arithmetic return or (2) the geometric return. The arithmetic return is the simple average return, which is calculated as the sum of the individual holding period returns divided by the number of returns.

Equation 10.2

$$\text{Arithmetic Return}(\bar{r_i}) = \frac{\sum_{i=1}^{n} HPR_i}{n}$$

The geometric return, on the other hand, is the compound average return.

Equation 10.3

Geometric Return = $[(1 + HPR_1) \times (1 + HPR_2) \times (1 + HPR_n)]^{1/n} - 1$

Although less common, the geometric return provides a better measure of the actual return received over time. To see why, consider the following example: Assume that Amanda bought Urban Outfitters on September 26, 2002 for $23. The stock increased to $26.50 on September 26, 2003. It fell to $23 on September 26, 2004, when she sold the stock. How much did Amanda earn on the investment? Obviously, she earned 0 percent. She bought it for $23 and sold it for $23 two years later.

$$HPR_1 = \frac{\$26.50 - \$23.00 + \$0}{\$23.00} \qquad HPR_2 = \frac{\$23.00 - \$26.50 + \$0}{\$26.50}$$

$$= 15.22\% \qquad\qquad\qquad = -13.21\%$$

$$\text{Arithmetic Return} = \frac{15.22 + (-13.21)}{2}$$

$$= 1\%$$

Geometric Average = $[(1.1522) \times (.8679)]^{1/2} - 1$

$$= 0\%$$

Although the arithmetic return is frequently reported, it does not provide a true measure of the return generated on the security; the arithmetic return in this case is 1 percent (which, of course, is incorrect). The geometric return (0 percent) provides a more accurate representation of the return generated on the investment.

10.2 Measures of Risk

Standard Deviation

Like return, there are two basic measures of risk: standard deviation and beta. Standard deviation is a statistical measure of the variability around the expected (or mean) return. The higher the variability, the higher the risk associated with that security. It is calculated as the square root of the variance; see *Equation 10.5*. In turn, variance is the squared difference between the actual return and the mean return; see *Equation 10.4*.

Equation 10.4

$$\sigma_m^2 = \frac{\sum_{i=1}^{n}\left(r_i - \overline{r_i}\right)}{n-1}$$

Equation 10.5

$$\sigma_m = \sqrt{\sigma^2} = \left(\sigma^2\right)^{\frac{1}{2}}$$

Standard deviation is a measure of total risk, which is the combination of systematic (or non-diversifiable) risk and unsystematic (or diversifiable) risk. Systematic risk is the risk of the "system" or market. It includes changes in interest rates, inflation rates, and other world events that affect all securities. Unfortunately, these risks cannot be diversified away. By contrast, unsystematic risk is risk specific to the company or industry in which the company operates. These risks can be diversified away, provided the investor holds 18 – 40 securities in his or her portfolio.

Let's consider an example. The holding period return on DPG Oil's stock over the past five years was calculated using the historical prices; see *Figure 10.4*. With this information, the arithmetic return and standard deviation of returns for the security can be calculated as follows:

$$\text{Return} = \frac{0.04 + 0.06 + (-0.08) + 0.10 + 0.12}{5}$$

$$= 0.0480$$

$$SD = \sqrt{\frac{(.04-.048)^2 + (.06-.048)^2 + (-.08-.048)^2 + (.10-.048)^2 + (.12-.048)^2}{(5-1)}}$$

$$= 0.0782$$

Figure 10.4 Holding Period Returns

Year	Return
1	0.04
2	0.06
3	-0.08
4	0.10
5	0.12

According to the Central Limit Theorum, if a sample includes at least 30 data points, the distribution is assumed to be normal. The Emperical Rule states that if the distribution is normal (i.e, bell shaped), then the average returns will fall at the peak of the distribution and a level of confidence for future returns can be derived by moving 1, 2, or 3 standard deviations from the mean. Specifically, there is a 68% level of confidence that future returns will fall within ± 1 standard deviation of the mean. Likewise, the level of confidence increases to 95% for ± 2 standard deviations and 99.7% for ± 3 standard deviations. In this case, there is a 95 percent chance that next year's returns will fall between 10.84 percent [4.8% - (2 x 7.82%)] and 20.44 percent [4.8% + (2 x 7.82%)], given the information provided above.

Beta Coefficient

As noted in Chapters 6 and 9, beta is a regression measure used to evaluate the riskiness of an individual security in relation to the overall market. The beta for the market (i.e., S&P 500) is 1.0. If an equity security has a beta of 2.0, it is twice as risky as the broad market. The mathematical formula for beta is the covariance (or movement) between the security and the overall market divided by the variance on the market.

Equation 10.5

$$\beta_i = \frac{COV(r_i, r_M)}{\sigma_M^2}$$

Beta provides a measure of systematic risk so it is only applicable to investments that are part of a diversified portfolio.

By calculating the various measures of risk and return outlined in this chapter, you will be able to evaluate the risk profile of a company. The calculations will also help you better understand the impact of managements' investment decisions on the risk/return characteristics of the company.

END OF CHAPTER PROBLEMS

Questions and Problems
Chapter 10

1. Total risk equals

    A. Systematic plus non-systematic risk
    B. Non-systematic plus diversifiable risk
    C. Non-systematic minus diversifiable risk
    D. Systematic risk plus non-diversifiable risk
    E. Systematic risk minus non-diversifiable risk

2. Which of the following is true about risk and return?
    A. Riskier assets will, on average, earn lower returns
    B. Based on historical data, there is no reward for bearing risk
    C. An increase in the risk of an investment will result in a decreased risk premium
    D. The reward for bearing risk is known as the standard deviation
    E. In general, the higher the expected return the higher the risk

3. Which of the following is likely to be associated with the lowest level of risk?

    A. Long-term government bonds
    B. U.S. Treasury bills
    C. Intermediate-term government bonds
    D. Common stock of the largest companies in the U.S.
    E. Common stock of the smallest companies in the U.S.

Use the following information on Barr Industries' stock to answer the next two questions.

Year	Return
1	0.04
2	0.06
3	0.08
4	0.10
5	0.12

4. What is the expected (arithmetic mean) return for the security?

   A. 6.00%
   B. 7.00%
   C. 8.00%
   D. 9.00%
   E. 10.00%

5. What is the standard deviation of returns for the security?

   A. 1.24%
   B. 2.75%
   C. 3.16%
   D. 4.35%
   E. 5.87%

6. A _____ distribution is symmetric, has a bell-shaped density curve with a single peak, and can be defined completely by its means and standard deviation.

   A. gamma
   B. Poisson
   C. binomial
   D. normal
   E. uniform

7. A domestic asset's return on investment has two components. The component that reflects the dividend(s) an investor receives while holding the asset is known as:

   A. the capital gain component
   B. the income component
   C. the total dollar return
   D. the percentage return
   E. None of the above

8. Melissa purchased a bond one year ago for $871. One interest payment of $90 was received during the year. If she sells the bond today for $950, what would be her total percentage return?

   A. 8.3%
   B. 11.1%
   C. 18.0%
   D. 19.4%
   E. 23.8%

Use the following information to answer the next 2 questions.

You purchased 500 shares of a stock at a price of $22.50 per share. One year later, the shares sold for $21 each. At that end of the year, a $1.50 per share dividend was paid. (Use this information to answer the next two questions).

9. What is the total dollar return for the investment?

   A. $0
   B. $750
   C. $1,250
   D. $1,500
   E. $1,750

10. What is the total percentage return for the investment?

    A. -7.1%
    B. –6.7%
    C. 0.0%
    D. 6.7%
    E. 7.1%

Financial Management: A Practical Guide to Value Creation

CASE ANALYSIS

Calculating Risk and Return
Case 10.1

Often times, the risk and return on a security are not provided. On the contrary, it must be calculated using historical price data. This case is demonstrates the process of taking raw price data and using it to determine the risk-return characteristics of a publicly traded company.

1. **Holding Period Return**

$$HPR(r) = \frac{P_1 - P_0 + CF}{P_0}$$

To calculate the Holding Period Return (HPR) for each period, use Excel as follows:

A. Download historical closing prices for a publicly traded security (e.g., URBN) and the broad market (i.e., .SPX). Pricing data can typically be acquired on a daily (2 years), weekly (5 years), and monthly (10 years) basis.

B. Insert a blank column next to the closing prices. This empty column will be used to calculate Holding Period Returns for each period (e.g., daily, weekly, or monthly). Assuming that you have downloaded monthly data for the last ten years, select the blank cell next to the second monthly closing price. For instance, if the data begins with January 1994, then select a blank cell next to the closing price for February 1994. Type in the formula for calculating HPR in the cell selected. For Example in cell C4 type: = (B4 – B3)/B3.

Copy and Paste this formula in the remaining empty cells to arrive at the HPRs for each month.

2. **Arithmetic (or Average) Return**

$$\text{Arithmetic Return}(\bar{r_i}) = \frac{\sum_{i=1}^{n} HPR_i}{n}$$

The Arithmetic Return can be calculated in two ways:

A. Sum of individual HPRs and divide by the number of returns

B. Select a cell where you want your average return to be displayed, click the paste function (f_x) on the toolbar, select AVERAGE from the STATISTICAL function category, and click OK. In the gray input box select all the individual HPRs and click OK.

3. **Annualized Return**

Now that you have calculated the average monthly return, you must convert it to an annual rate. To annualize the return, select the cell where you would like the annualized return to be displayed and use the formula provided below.

$$E(R_i) = (1 + \bar{r_i})^m - 1$$

where m represents the frequency of the data (e.g., daily, weekly, or monthly). For instance, if monthly data was used, m = 12.

4. Standard Deviation

Standard deviation is a measure of variability around the expected value calculated by taking the square root of the variance. Standard deviation can be computed in one of two ways:

A. To compute standard deviation manually, insert a column next to the HPR. Then, calculate the squared difference between the individual holding period return (r_i) and the average return calculated above. Copy and paste this formula into each empty cell. At the bottom of the column, sum the squared differences and divide by n-1, with n-1 being the number of HPR minus 1. This will give you a measure of the squared deviations around the mean, or variance. In the next cell, calculate the square root of the variance to arrive at the standard deviation.

B. Select a cell where you want standard deviation to be displayed, click the paste function (f_x) on the Excel toolbar, select STDEV from the STATISTICAL function category, and click OK. In the gray input box select all the periodic HPRs and click OK. This function will return the standard deviation for the period.

$$\sigma_m^2 = \frac{\sum_{i=1}^{n}\left(r_i - \overline{r_i}\right)}{n-1}$$

$$\sigma_m = \sqrt{\sigma^2} = \left(\sigma^2\right)^{\frac{1}{2}}$$

5. **Annualized Standard Deviation**

$$\sigma_A = \sigma_m \sqrt{m}$$

The annualized standard deviation is calculated by multiplying the periodic standard deviation by the square root of the period, m. For instance, if the data downloaded from Reuters was monthly, then the monthly standard deviation figure calculated above would be multiplied by the square root of 12.

The Emperical Rule states that if the distribution is normal (i.e, bell shaped), the the Average Return would fall at the peak of the distribution and a level of confidence for future returns could be derived by moving 1, 2, or 3 standard deviations from the mean. Specifically, there is a 68% level of confidence that future returns will fall within ± 1 standard deviation of the mean. Likewise, the level of confidence increases to 95% for ±2 standard deviations and 99.7% for ±3 standard deviations.

6. **Beta**

Beta is a regression measure used to evaluate the riskiness of an individual security in relation to the overall market. The beta for the market (i.e., the S&P 500) is 1.0. The mathematical formula for beta is the covariance (or movement) between the security and the overall market divided by the variance on the market, or:

$$\beta_i = \frac{COV(r_i, r_M)}{\sigma_M^2}$$

Beta can be determined in one of two ways:

A. Select a cell where you want covariance to be displayed, click the paste function (f$_x$) on the Excel toolbar, select COVAR from the STATISTICAL function category, and click OK. In the gray input box select all the periodic HPRs for the security (array 1) and the broad market (array 2) and click OK. This function will return the covariance between the security and the overall market. Then, select the cell where you want beta to be displayed and enter the formula provided above.

B. On the Excel toolbar, click Tools and select Data Analysis from the drop down menu. In the Regression box, you must select the X and Y range. Y is the dependent variable (i.e., the return on the individual security) and X is the independent variable (i.e., the return on the market). Highlight the cells displaying the holding period returns for the security (Y) and the broad market (X). Then, click the radio button for Output range, select the area where you want the results to be displayed, and click OK.

7. **Sharpe Ratio**

$$S_p = \frac{(E(R_p) - r_f)}{\sigma_p}$$

The Sharpe Ratio is a measure of risk-adjusted return. Unfortunately, there is no function in Excel to calculate the Sharpe Ratio. You will need to use the formula indicated above and reference to the cells dynamically. For simplicity, assume that the risk free rate (r$_f$) = 5%.

Repeat the same procedure using the historical prices for the S&P 500 (.SPX) and then compare the two ratios. The Sharpe ratio is a comparative measure; the security with the highest Sharpe ratio provides the highest level of risk-adjusted return.

Figure A101.1 illustrates how the pricing data can be used to calculate the individual monthly holding period returns.

Figure A101.1 Calculation of Holding Period Return

Date	URBN		SPX	
	Close	HPR	Close	HPR
Jan-24-2003	20.89	-0.022919	927.57	0.02089
Jan-31-2003	20.48	-0.019627	901.78	-0.0278
Feb-7-2003	19.92	-0.027344	861.4	-0.04478
Feb-14-2003	18.72	-0.060241	855.7	-0.00662
Feb-21-2003	17.74	-0.05235	829.69	-0.0304
Feb-28-2003	18.93	0.06708	834.89	0.006267
Mar-7-2003	19.81	0.046487	848.17	0.015906
Mar-14-2003	22.92	0.156991	841.15	-0.00828
Mar-21-2003	24.86	0.084642	828.89	-0.01458
Mar-28-2003	22.79	-0.083266	833.27	0.005284
Apr-4-2003	24.2	0.061869	895.79	0.07503
Apr-11-2003	25.41	0.05	863.5	-0.03605
Apr-18-2003	25.71	0.011806	878.85	0.017776
Apr-25-2003	28.49	0.108129	868.3	-0.012
May-2-2003	29.71	0.042822	893.58	0.029114
May-9-2003	30.75	0.035005	898.81	0.005853
May-16-2003	31.99	0.040325	930.08	0.03479
May-23-2003	31.911	-0.00247	933.41	0.00358
May-30-2003	33.32	0.044154	944.3	0.011667
Jun-6-2003	36.69	0.10114	933.22	-0.01173

Figure A101.2 illustrates the results of the analysis based on data extending from 06/01/93 to 06/01/03.

Figure A101.2 Risk and Return

		URBN.O	.SPX
Weekly Return	=	0.0080	-0.0002
Annual Return	=	0.5131	-0.0108
Weekly Standard Deviation	=	0.0964	0.0291
Annual Standard Deviation	=	0.6949	0.2096
Beta	=	0.5916	0.9961
Sharpe Ratio	=	0.6664	-0.2903

APPENDIX A
MATHEMATICAL FORMULAS

Chapter 2 Financial Statements

Income (Loss) = Revenue − Expenses

$$\text{Earnings per share (EPS)} = \frac{\text{Net Income}}{\text{Shares Outstanding}}$$

$$\text{Average Tax Rate} = \frac{\text{Total Taxes Paid}}{\text{Taxable Income}}$$

Assets = Liabilities + Owner's Equity

Cash Flow = Operating Activities + Investing Activities
          + Financing Activities

Chapter 3 Financial Statement Analysis

Cash Flow from Assets = Operating Cash Flow − Capital Spending
          − Changes NWC

Operating Cash Flow = EBIT + Depreciation − Taxes

Capital Spending = Ending Net Fixed Assets − Beginning Net Fixed Assets + Depreciation

Changes in Net Working Capital (NWC) = Ending NWC − Beginning NWC

Net Operating Working Capital = (Cash + AR + INV) − (AP + Accruals)

Net Operating Profit After Taxes (NOPAT) = EBIT x (1 − Tax Rate)

Operating Cash Flow (OCF) = NOPAT + Depreciation

Net Investment in Operating Capital (NIOC) = Operating Capital $_1$ − Operating Capital $_0$

Gross Investment in Operating Capital = NIOC + Depreciation

Free Cash Flow = Operating Cash Flow − Gross Investment in Operating Capital

$$\text{Current Ratio} = \frac{\text{Current Assets}}{\text{Current Liabilities}}$$

$$\text{Quick Ratio} = \frac{\text{Current Assets} - \text{Inventory}}{\text{Current Liabilities}}$$

$$\text{Total Debt Ratio} = \frac{\text{Total Assets} - \text{Total Equity}}{\text{Total Assets}}$$

$$\text{Debt} - \text{Equity Ratio} = \frac{\text{Total Debt}}{\text{Total Equity}}$$

$$\text{Times Interest Earned Ratio} = \frac{\text{EBIT}}{\text{Interest Expense}}$$

$$\text{Inventory Turnover} = \frac{\text{Cost of Goods Sold}}{\text{Inventory}}$$

$$\text{Days' Sales in Inventory} = \frac{365 \text{ days}}{\text{Inventory Turnover}}$$

$$\text{Receivables Turnover} = \frac{\text{Sales}}{\text{Accounts Receivable}}$$

$$\text{Days' Sales in Receivables} = \frac{365 \text{ days}}{\text{Receivables Turnover}}$$

$$\text{Asset Turnover} = \frac{\text{Sales}}{\text{Total Assets}}$$

$$\text{Gross Margin} = \frac{(\text{Sales} - \text{Costs of Goods Sold})}{\text{Sales}}$$

$$\text{Operating Margin} = \frac{\text{Income Before Taxes (EBT)}}{\text{Sales}}$$

$$\text{Net Profit Margin} = \frac{\text{Net Income}}{\text{Sales}}$$

$$\text{Return on Assets} = \frac{\text{Net Income}}{\text{Total Assets}}$$

$$\text{Return on Equity} = \frac{\text{Net Income}}{\text{Total Equity}}$$

$$\text{Dividend Payout Ratio} = \frac{\text{Cash Dividend}}{\text{Net Income}}$$

$$\text{Retention Ratio} = \frac{\text{Addition to Retained Earnings}}{\text{Net Income}}$$

$$\text{Internal Growth Rate} = \frac{\text{ROA} \times b}{1 - \text{ROA} \times b}$$

$$\text{Sustainable Growth Rate} = \frac{\text{ROE} \times b}{1 - \text{ROE} \times b}$$

Chapter 4 Financial Forecasting

External Funds Needed (EFN) = Projected Total Assets − Projected Total Liabilities & Equity

Chapter 5 Time Value of Money: Lump Sum Cash Flows

$$FV = PV(1 + I\%)^N$$

$$FV = PV\left(1 + \frac{I\%}{m}\right)^{N \times m}$$

$$PV = \frac{FV}{(1 + I\%)^N}$$

$$PV = \frac{FV}{\left(1 + \frac{I\%}{m}\right)^{N \times m}}$$

Simple Interest = Present Value x Interest x Number of Periods

Chapter 6 Time Value of Money: Multiple Cash Flows

$$PV_A = PMT \times \left(\frac{1 - \text{Present Value Factor}}{I\%} \right)$$

$$= PMT \times \left\{ \frac{1 - [1/(1+I\%)^N]}{I\%} \right\}$$

$PV_{AD} = PV_A (1 + I\%)$

$$FV_A = (\text{Future Value Factor} - 1)/I\%$$

$$= [(1+I\%)^N - 1]/I\%$$

$FV_{AD} = FV_A (1 + I\%)$

$$PV = PMT \times \left\{ \frac{1 - \left[\frac{1}{(1+I\%)^N} \right]}{I\%} \right\} + \frac{FV}{(1+I\%)^N}$$

$$PV = \frac{PMT}{2} \times \left\{ \frac{1 - \left[\dfrac{1}{\left(1 + \dfrac{I\%}{2}\right)^{N \times 2}}\right]}{\dfrac{I\%}{2}} \right\} + \frac{FV}{\left(1 + \dfrac{I\%}{2}\right)^{N \times 2}}$$

$$P_0 = \left(\frac{D}{I\%}\right)$$

$$P_0 = \left[\frac{D_0(1+g)}{(I\% - g)}\right] = \frac{D_1}{(I\% - g)}$$

$$\text{Price/earningsMultiple} = \frac{\text{Current PricePerShare}}{\text{EarningsPerShare}}$$

Chapter 7 Capital Budgeting: Decision Rules

$$NPV = -C_0 + \sum_{N=1} \frac{CF_N}{(1 + I\%)^N}$$

$$PI = \frac{\sum_{t=1} \dfrac{CF_t}{(1+k)^t}}{I_0}$$

Financial Management: A Practical Guide to Value Creation   269

Chapter 8: Capital Budgeting: Cash Flow Projections

Project Cash Flows = Initial Investment + Operating Cash Flow
         + Terminal Cash Flow

Initial Investment = Installed Cost of a New Asset
         − After-tax Proceeds from the Sale of the Old Asset
         + Changes in Net Working Capital

Installed Cost of a New Asset = Acquisition Costs + Installation Costs

After-tax Proceeds from Old Asset = Sale Proceeds from Old Asset
         +/− Taxes on the Sale of Old Asset

Operating Cash Flow = EBIT + Depreciation − Taxes

Terminal Cash Flow = After-tax Proceeds from Sale of New Asset
         − After-tax Proceeds from Sale of Old Asset
         +/− Changes in Net Working Capital

Chapter 9: Capital Budgeting: Cost of Capital

Coupon Rate = Annual Coupon / Face Value

Current Yield = Annual Coupon / Current Price

$$R_E = \frac{D_1}{P_0} + g$$

$$R_E = R_f + \beta_E \times (R_M - R_f)$$

$$\beta = \frac{Cov_{E,M}}{\sigma_E \sigma_M}$$

$$R_P = \frac{D}{P_0}$$

$$WACC = (E/V)R_E + [(D/V)R_D(1-T)] + (P/V)R_P$$

$$BP_i = \frac{F_i}{w_i}$$

Chapter 10 Risk and Return

$$HPR = \frac{P_1 - P_0 + CF}{P_0}$$

$$\text{Arithmetic Return}(\bar{r_i}) = \frac{\sum_{i=1}^{n} HPR_i}{n}$$

Geometric Return = $[(1 + HPR_1) \times (1 + HPR_2) \times (1 + HPR_N)]^{1/N} - 1$

$$\sigma_m^2 = \frac{\sum_{i=1}^{n}(r_i - \bar{r_i})}{n-1} \qquad \sigma_m = \sqrt{\sigma^2}$$

$$\beta = \frac{Cov_{E,M}}{\sigma_E \sigma_M}$$

APPENDIX B
CALCULATOR KEYSTROKES

HP-10B Financial Calculator

Settings

End Mode and Begin Mode

In most problems, payment is made at the end of a period, and this is the default setting (end mode) for the HP-10B. Annuities due assume payments are made at the beginning of each period (begin mode). On the HP-10B, pressing Beg/End toggles between begin and end mode.

Compounding Frequency

The HP-10B is hardwired to assume annual compounding. To change this default setting, press 1 P/YR. To verify that the default has been changed, press the key, then press and briefly hold the INPUT key.

Sign Changes (Cash Inflows and Outflows)

Sign changes are used to identify the direction of cash inflows and outflows. Generally, cash inflows are entered as positive numbers and cash outflows are entered as negative numbers. To enter a negative number on the HP-10B, press the appropriate digit keys and then press the change sign key +/-.

Calculations

Future Value of a Lump Sum

What is the future value of $7,500 invested at for 10 years at an annual rate of 15 percent?

1 P/YR	
7,500 +/-	PV
10	■ N
15	I%
FV	30,341.68

The future value is $30,341.68.

What is the future value of $7,500 invested for 10 years at a rate of 15 percent compounded quarterly?

4	P/YR
7,500 +/-	PV
10	■ N
15	I%
FV	32,702.84

The future value is $32,702.84.

Present value of a Lump Sum

If you need $40,000 to start a new business in 5 years and you can earn a rate of 12 percent on your investable funds, how much do you need to set aside today to meet your goal?

Financial Management: A Practical Guide to Value Creation

```
1 P/YR
40,000 +/-    FV
5             ■ N
12            I%
PV            22,697.07
```

The present value is $22,697.07.

If you need $40,000 to start a new business in 5 years and you can earn a rate of 12 percent compounded monthly, how much do you need to set aside today to meet your goal?

```
12 P/YR
40,000 +/-    FV
5             ■ N
12            I%
PV            $22,017.97
```

The present value is $22,017.97.

Future Value of an Ordinary Annuity

If you contribute $2,000 to your Roth IRA every year for the next 20 years and earn an annual rate of 8% return, how much will you have for retirement?

```
1 P/YR
2,000 +/-     PMT
20            N
8             I%
FV            91,523.92
```

The future value is $91,523.92.

Future Value of an Annuity Due

If you put $2,500 into a 401(k) earning 9% annual interest on the first business day of each year for the next 25 years, how much would you have at the end of 25 years?

1 P/YR
2,500 +/-   PMT
9   I%
25   N
FV   230,809.94

The future value is $230,809.94.

Present Value of an Annuity

What is the present value of a $1,000 par value bond with a coupon payment of $100 and 5 years to maturity, when the market interest rate is 7%?

1 P/YR
100   PMT
1000   FV
5   N
7   I
PV   -1,123.00

The present value is $1,123.00.

Present Value of an Annuity Due

What amount must you invest today a 6% interest rate compounded annually so that you can withdraw $5,000 at the beginning of each year for the next 5 years?

1 P/YR	
5,000	PMT
6	I
5	N
PV	22,325.53

The present value is equal to $22,325.53.

Annuity Payment

What is the annual payment on a $100,000, 10-year loan issued at a rate of 7% compounded annually?

1 P/YR	
100,000	PV
7	I
10	■ N
PMT	14,237.75

The annual loan payment would be $14,237.75.

What is the annual payment on a $100,000, 10-year loan issued at a rate of 7% compounded monthly?

12 P/YR	
100,000	PV
7	I
10	∎ N
PMT	1,161.08

The annual loan payment would be $1,161.08.

Loan Amortization

Prepare an amortization schedule for a 3 year loan of $25,000. The interest rate on the loan is 12% per year and the loan calls for annual payments. How much interest is paid in the 2nd year and how much interest is paid over the course of the loan?

-25,000	PV
12	I/YR
3	N
PMT	10,408.72

The payment would be $10,408.72.

∎ AMORT = Principal of $8,297.77, =Interest of $2,110.95 = Balance of $6,226.15.

Interest Paid = ($10,408.72 x 3) - $25,000 = $6,226.15

Interest Rate (lump sum calculation)

Assume you want to retire in 25 years with a nest egg of $1 million and you have $25,000 to invest, what rate of return will you need to achieve to reach your goal?

```
1 P/YR
25,000 +/-      PV
25              N
1,000,000       FV
I%              15.89%
```

The required rate of return is 15.89%.

Interest Rate (annuity calculation)

If you need $15,000 in 10 years, and you are willing to invest $1,000 annually, what interest rate is required?

```
1,000 +/-       PMT
10              N
15,000          FV
I%              8.73%
```

The annuity would have to earn 8.73% annually.

Compounding Period (lump sum calculation)

If you invest $2,500 at 5%, how long will it take to double your money?

```
2,500 +/-       PV
5,000           FV
5               I%
N               14.21
```

Your money will double in 14.21 years.

Compounding Period (annuity calculation)

$15,000 is needed sometime in the future. How long, investing $1,000 per year, earning 9 percent annually, would it take to amass this amount of money?

1 P/YR	
15,000 +/-	FV
1,000	PMT
9	I%
N	9.91

It would take 9.91 years to earn $15,000.

Bond Valuation

A company issued 10 year bonds one year ago with a coupon rate of 8%. If the bonds make semiannual payments and the YTM on the bonds is 7%, what is the current price of the bond?

2 P/YR	
40.00	PMT
1,000	FV
9	N
7	I%
PV	-1,065.95

The current bond price is $1,065.95.

Yield to Maturity

A company issues 10% coupon bonds with 10 years until maturity. The bonds make annual payments and currently sell for $1,200.00, what is the YTM?

1 P/YR	
1,200 +/-	PV
100	PMT
1,000	FV
10	■ N
I%	7.13

The YTM is 7.13%.

Cash Flow Analysis

What is the net present value and internal rate of return for the following set of cash flows? Assume a discount rate of 10 %.

Year	Cash Flow
0	-$1,000
1	100
2	500
3	1,000

1,000 +/-	CFj
100	CFj
500	CFj
1,000	CFj
10	I/YR
NPV	255.44

The project has a NPV of $255.44.

What is the net present value and internal rate of return for the following set of cash flows? Assume a discount rate of 10 %.

Year	Cash Flow
4	-$1,000
5	100
6	500
7	1,000

1,000 +/-	CFj
500	CFj
3	Nj
10	I/YR
NPV	243.43

The project has a NPV of $243.43.

APPENDIX C
FINANCIAL WEBSITES

Business Plans

BusinessPlans.com	http://www.bplans.com/contentkit/qindex.cfm?affiliate=quicken
BusinessPlans.org	http://www.businessplans.org
Entrepreneur.com	http://www.entrepreneur.com/howto/bizplan/0,5971,,00.html
Quicken.com	http://www.quicken.com/cms/viewers/article/small_business/50279
Small Business Administration	http://www.sba.gov/starting_business/planning/basic.html

Company Data

BigCharts	http://www.bigcharts.com
EComp Online	http://www.ecomponline.com
Earnings	http://www.earnings.com
Stocks	http://www.stocks.com
US SEC	http://www.sec.gov

Financial Calculators

Bloomberg Calculators	http://www.bloomberg.com/analysis/calculators/currency.html
CNN Money Moneyville	http://money.cnn.com/pf/saving/moneyville
Java Calculators	http://www.dinkytown.com

Financial Dictionaries

Bloomberg Financial Glossary	http://www.bloomberg.com/analysis/glossary/bfglosa.htm
Investopedia	http://www.investopedia.com
InvestorWords	http://www.investorwords.com
Motley Fool Glossary	http://www.fool.com/school/Glossary/glossary.htm
Yahoo! Financial Dictionaries	http://biz.yahoo.com/edu/

Financial Markets

Bloomberg	http://www.bloomberg.com
Morningstar	http://www.morningstar.com
MSN MoneyCentral	http://moneycentral.msn.com http://www.cnbc.com
MultexNet	http://www.marketguide.com

CNN Money	http://money.cnn.com
Yahoo! Finance	http://finance.yahoo.com

Financial Ratios

American Express	http://home3.americanexpress.com/smallbusiness/tool/ratios/financialratio.asp
Biz/ed	http://www.bized.ac.uk/compfact/ratios/
Business.com	http://www.business.com/directory/accounting/financial_statements/financial_ratios/
Investopedia	http://www.investopedia.com

Finance Tutorials

Bloomberg University	http://www.bloomberg.com/analysis/univ/index.html
Investopedia Tutorials	http://www.investopedia.com/university/
Morningstar Learning Center	http://www.morningstar.com/centers/Learning.html?pfsection=learningctr
MSN MoneyCentral	http://moneycentral.msn.com/content/newtoday.asp
Motley Fool's School	http://www.fool.com/school.htm
CNN Money 101	http://money.cnn.com/pf/101/

APPENDIX D
TVM TABLES

FV of Lump Sum (at I%, N periods)

Period	1%	2%	3%	4%	5%	6%	7%	8%	9%	10%
1	1.010	1.020	1.030	1.040	1.050	1.060	1.070	1.080	1.090	1.100
2	1.020	1.040	1.061	1.082	1.103	1.124	1.145	1.166	1.188	1.210
3	1.030	1.061	1.093	1.125	1.158	1.191	1.225	1.260	1.295	1.331
4	1.041	1.082	1.126	1.170	1.216	1.262	1.311	1.360	1.412	1.464
5	1.051	1.104	1.159	1.217	1.276	1.338	1.403	1.469	1.539	1.611
6	1.062	1.126	1.194	1.265	1.340	1.419	1.501	1.587	1.677	1.772
7	1.072	1.149	1.230	1.316	1.407	1.504	1.606	1.714	1.828	1.949
8	1.083	1.172	1.267	1.369	1.477	1.594	1.718	1.851	1.993	2.144
9	1.094	1.195	1.305	1.423	1.551	1.689	1.838	1.999	2.172	2.358
10	1.105	1.219	1.344	1.480	1.629	1.791	1.967	2.159	2.367	2.594
11	1.116	1.243	1.384	1.539	1.710	1.898	2.105	2.332	2.580	2.853
12	1.127	1.268	1.426	1.601	1.796	2.012	2.252	2.518	2.813	3.138
13	1.138	1.294	1.469	1.665	1.886	2.133	2.410	2.720	3.066	3.452
14	1.149	1.319	1.513	1.732	1.980	2.261	2.579	2.937	3.342	3.797
15	1.161	1.346	1.558	1.801	2.079	2.397	2.759	3.172	3.642	4.177
16	1.173	1.373	1.605	1.873	2.183	2.540	2.952	3.426	3.970	4.595
17	1.184	1.400	1.653	1.948	2.292	2.693	3.159	3.700	4.328	5.054
18	1.196	1.428	1.702	2.026	2.407	2.854	3.380	3.996	4.717	5.560
19	1.208	1.457	1.754	2.107	2.527	3.026	3.617	4.316	5.142	6.116
20	1.220	1.486	1.806	2.191	2.653	3.207	3.870	4.661	5.604	6.727

Period	11%	12%	13%	14%	15%	16%	17%	18%	19%	20%
1	1.110	1.120	1.130	1.140	1.150	1.160	1.170	1.180	1.190	1.200
2	1.232	1.254	1.277	1.300	1.323	1.346	1.369	1.392	1.416	1.440
3	1.368	1.405	1.443	1.482	1.521	1.561	1.602	1.643	1.685	1.728
4	1.518	1.574	1.630	1.689	1.749	1.811	1.874	1.939	2.005	2.074
5	1.685	1.762	1.842	1.925	2.011	2.100	2.192	2.288	2.386	2.488
6	1.870	1.974	2.082	2.195	2.313	2.436	2.565	2.700	2.840	2.986
7	2.076	2.211	2.353	2.502	2.660	2.826	3.001	3.185	3.379	3.583
8	2.305	2.476	2.658	2.853	3.059	3.278	3.511	3.759	4.021	4.300
9	2.558	2.773	3.004	3.252	3.518	3.803	4.108	4.435	4.785	5.160
10	2.839	3.106	3.395	3.707	4.046	4.411	4.807	5.234	5.695	6.192
11	3.152	3.479	3.836	4.226	4.652	5.117	5.624	6.176	6.777	7.430
12	3.498	3.896	4.335	4.818	5.350	5.936	6.580	7.288	8.064	8.916
13	3.883	4.363	4.898	5.492	6.153	6.886	7.699	8.599	9.596	10.699
14	4.310	4.887	5.535	6.261	7.076	7.988	9.007	10.147	11.420	12.839
15	4.785	5.474	6.254	7.138	8.137	9.266	10.539	11.974	13.590	15.407
16	5.311	6.130	7.067	8.137	9.358	10.748	12.330	14.129	16.172	18.488
17	5.895	6.866	7.986	9.276	10.761	12.468	14.426	16.672	19.244	22.186
18	6.544	7.690	9.024	10.575	12.375	14.463	16.879	19.673	22.901	26.623
19	7.263	8.613	10.197	12.056	14.232	16.777	19.748	23.214	27.252	31.948
20	8.062	9.646	11.523	13.743	16.367	19.461	23.106	27.393	32.429	38.338

Financial Management: A Practical Guide to Value Creation 287

Present Value of a Lump Sum (at I%, N periods)

Period	1%	2%	3%	4%	5%	6%	7%	8%	9%	10%
1	0.990	0.980	0.971	0.962	0.952	0.943	0.935	0.926	0.917	0.909
2	0.980	0.961	0.943	0.925	0.907	0.890	0.873	0.857	0.842	0.826
3	0.971	0.942	0.915	0.889	0.864	0.840	0.816	0.794	0.772	0.751
4	0.961	0.924	0.888	0.855	0.823	0.792	0.763	0.735	0.708	0.683
5	0.951	0.906	0.863	0.822	0.784	0.747	0.713	0.681	0.650	0.621
6	0.942	0.888	0.837	0.790	0.746	0.705	0.666	0.630	0.596	0.564
7	0.933	0.871	0.813	0.760	0.711	0.665	0.623	0.583	0.547	0.513
8	0.923	0.853	0.789	0.731	0.677	0.627	0.582	0.540	0.502	0.467
9	0.914	0.837	0.766	0.703	0.645	0.592	0.544	0.500	0.460	0.424
10	0.905	0.820	0.744	0.676	0.614	0.558	0.508	0.463	0.422	0.386
11	0.896	0.804	0.722	0.650	0.585	0.527	0.475	0.429	0.388	0.350
12	0.887	0.788	0.701	0.625	0.557	0.497	0.444	0.397	0.356	0.319
13	0.879	0.773	0.681	0.601	0.530	0.469	0.415	0.368	0.326	0.290
14	0.870	0.758	0.661	0.577	0.505	0.442	0.388	0.340	0.299	0.263
15	0.861	0.743	0.642	0.555	0.481	0.417	0.362	0.315	0.275	0.239
16	0.853	0.728	0.623	0.534	0.458	0.394	0.339	0.292	0.252	0.218
17	0.844	0.714	0.605	0.513	0.436	0.371	0.317	0.270	0.231	0.198
18	0.836	0.700	0.587	0.494	0.416	0.350	0.296	0.250	0.212	0.180
19	0.828	0.686	0.570	0.475	0.396	0.331	0.277	0.232	0.194	0.164
20	0.820	0.673	0.554	0.456	0.377	0.312	0.258	0.215	0.178	0.149

Period	11%	12%	13%	14%	15%	16%	17%	18%	19%	20%
1	0.901	0.893	0.885	0.877	0.870	0.862	0.855	0.847	0.840	0.833
2	0.812	0.797	0.783	0.769	0.756	0.743	0.731	0.718	0.706	0.694
3	0.731	0.712	0.693	0.675	0.658	0.641	0.624	0.609	0.593	0.579
4	0.659	0.636	0.613	0.592	0.572	0.552	0.534	0.516	0.499	0.482
5	0.593	0.567	0.543	0.519	0.497	0.476	0.456	0.437	0.419	0.402
6	0.535	0.507	0.480	0.456	0.432	0.410	0.390	0.370	0.352	0.335
7	0.482	0.452	0.425	0.400	0.376	0.354	0.333	0.314	0.296	0.279
8	0.434	0.404	0.376	0.351	0.327	0.305	0.285	0.266	0.249	0.233
9	0.391	0.361	0.333	0.308	0.284	0.263	0.243	0.225	0.209	0.194
10	0.352	0.322	0.295	0.270	0.247	0.227	0.208	0.191	0.176	0.162
11	0.317	0.287	0.261	0.237	0.215	0.195	0.178	0.162	0.148	0.135
12	0.286	0.257	0.231	0.208	0.187	0.168	0.152	0.137	0.124	0.112
13	0.258	0.229	0.204	0.182	0.163	0.145	0.130	0.116	0.104	0.093
14	0.232	0.205	0.181	0.160	0.141	0.125	0.111	0.099	0.088	0.078
15	0.209	0.183	0.160	0.140	0.123	0.108	0.095	0.084	0.074	0.065
16	0.188	0.163	0.141	0.123	0.107	0.093	0.081	0.071	0.062	0.054
17	0.170	0.146	0.125	0.108	0.093	0.080	0.069	0.060	0.052	0.045
18	0.153	0.130	0.111	0.095	0.081	0.069	0.059	0.051	0.044	0.038
19	0.138	0.116	0.098	0.083	0.070	0.060	0.051	0.043	0.037	0.031
20	0.124	0.104	0.087	0.073	0.061	0.051	0.043	0.037	0.031	0.026

Future Value of an Ordinary Annuity ($1 at I% for N periods)

Period	1%	2%	3%	4%	5%	6%	7%	8%	9%	10%
1	1.000	1.000	1.000	1.000	1.000	1.000	1.000	1.000	1.000	1.000
2	2.010	2.020	2.030	2.040	2.050	2.060	2.070	2.080	2.090	2.100
3	3.030	3.060	3.091	3.122	3.153	3.184	3.215	3.246	3.278	3.310
4	4.060	4.122	4.184	4.246	4.310	4.375	4.440	4.506	4.573	4.641
5	5.101	5.204	5.309	5.416	5.526	5.637	5.751	5.867	5.985	6.105
6	6.152	6.308	6.468	6.633	6.802	6.975	7.153	7.336	7.523	7.716
7	7.214	7.434	7.662	7.898	8.142	8.394	8.654	8.923	9.200	9.487
8	8.286	8.583	8.892	9.214	9.549	9.897	10.260	10.637	11.028	11.436
9	9.369	9.755	10.159	10.583	11.027	11.491	11.978	12.488	13.021	13.579
10	10.462	10.950	11.464	12.006	12.578	13.181	13.816	14.487	15.193	15.937
11	11.567	12.169	12.808	13.486	14.207	14.972	15.784	16.645	17.560	18.531
12	12.683	13.412	14.192	15.026	15.917	16.870	17.888	18.977	20.141	21.384
13	13.809	14.680	15.618	16.627	17.713	18.882	20.141	21.495	22.953	24.523
14	14.947	15.974	17.086	18.292	19.599	21.015	22.550	24.215	26.019	27.975
15	16.097	17.293	18.599	20.024	21.579	23.276	25.129	27.152	29.361	31.772
16	17.258	18.639	20.157	21.825	23.657	25.673	27.888	30.324	33.003	35.950
17	18.430	20.012	21.762	23.698	25.840	28.213	30.840	33.750	36.974	40.545
18	19.615	21.412	23.414	25.645	28.132	30.906	33.999	37.450	41.301	45.599
19	20.811	22.841	25.117	27.671	30.539	33.760	37.379	41.446	46.018	51.159
20	22.019	24.297	26.870	29.778	33.066	36.786	40.995	45.762	51.160	57.275

APPENDIX D TVM Tables

Period	11%	12%	13%	14%	15%	16%	17%	18%	19%	20%
1	1.000	1.000	1.000	1.000	1.000	1.000	1.000	1.000	1.000	1.000
2	2.110	2.120	2.130	2.140	2.150	2.160	2.170	2.180	2.190	2.200
3	3.342	3.374	3.407	3.440	3.473	3.506	3.539	3.572	3.606	3.640
4	4.710	4.779	4.850	4.921	4.993	5.066	5.141	5.215	5.291	5.368
5	6.228	6.353	6.480	6.610	6.742	6.877	7.014	7.154	7.297	7.442
6	7.913	8.115	8.323	8.536	8.754	8.977	9.207	9.442	9.683	9.930
7	9.783	10.089	10.405	10.730	11.067	11.414	11.772	12.142	12.523	12.916
8	11.859	12.300	12.757	13.233	13.727	14.240	14.773	15.327	15.902	16.499
9	14.164	14.776	15.416	16.085	16.786	17.519	18.285	19.086	19.923	20.799
10	16.722	17.549	18.420	19.337	20.304	21.321	22.393	23.521	24.709	25.959
11	19.561	20.655	21.814	23.045	24.349	25.733	27.200	28.755	30.404	32.150
12	22.713	24.133	25.650	27.271	29.002	30.850	32.824	34.931	37.180	39.581
13	26.212	28.029	29.985	32.089	34.352	36.786	39.404	42.219	45.244	48.497
14	30.095	32.393	34.883	37.581	40.505	43.672	47.103	50.818	54.841	59.196
15	34.405	37.280	40.417	43.842	47.580	51.660	56.110	60.965	66.261	72.035
16	39.190	42.753	46.672	50.980	55.717	60.925	66.649	72.939	79.850	87.442
17	44.501	48.884	53.739	59.118	65.075	71.673	78.979	87.068	96.022	105.93
18	50.396	55.750	61.725	68.394	75.836	84.141	93.406	103.74	115.27	128.12
19	56.939	63.440	70.749	78.969	88.212	98.603	110.28	123.41	138.17	154.74
20	64.203	72.052	80.947	91.025	102.44	115.38	130.03	146.63	165.42	186.69

Present Value of an Ordinary Annuity ($1 at I% for N periods)

Period	1%	2%	3%	4%	5%	6%	7%	8%	9%	10%
1	0.990	0.980	0.971	0.962	0.952	0.943	0.935	0.926	0.917	0.909
2	1.970	1.942	1.913	1.886	1.859	1.833	1.808	1.783	1.759	1.736
3	2.941	2.884	2.829	2.775	2.723	2.673	2.624	2.577	2.531	2.487
4	3.902	3.808	3.717	3.630	3.546	3.465	3.387	3.312	3.240	3.170
5	4.853	4.713	4.580	4.452	4.329	4.212	4.100	3.993	3.890	3.791
6	5.795	5.601	5.417	5.242	5.076	4.917	4.767	4.623	4.486	4.355
7	6.728	6.472	6.230	6.002	5.786	5.582	5.389	5.206	5.033	4.868
8	7.652	7.325	7.020	6.733	6.463	6.210	5.971	5.747	5.535	5.335
9	8.566	8.162	7.786	7.435	7.108	6.802	6.515	6.247	5.995	5.759
10	9.471	8.983	8.530	8.111	7.722	7.360	7.024	6.710	6.418	6.145
11	10.368	9.787	9.253	8.760	8.306	7.887	7.499	7.139	6.805	6.495
12	11.255	10.575	9.954	9.385	8.863	8.384	7.943	7.536	7.161	6.814
13	12.134	11.348	10.635	9.986	9.394	8.853	8.358	7.904	7.487	7.103
14	13.004	12.106	11.296	10.563	9.899	9.295	8.745	8.244	7.786	7.367
15	13.865	12.849	11.938	11.118	10.380	9.712	9.108	8.559	8.061	7.606
16	14.718	13.578	12.561	11.652	10.838	10.106	9.447	8.851	8.313	7.824
17	15.562	14.292	13.166	12.166	11.274	10.477	9.763	9.122	8.544	8.022
18	16.398	14.992	13.754	12.659	11.690	10.828	10.059	9.372	8.756	8.201
19	17.226	15.678	14.324	13.134	12.085	11.158	10.336	9.604	8.950	8.365
20	18.046	16.351	14.877	13.590	12.462	11.470	10.594	9.818	9.129	8.514

Period	11%	12%	13%	14%	15%	16%	17%	18%	19%	20%
1	0.901	0.893	0.885	0.877	0.870	0.862	0.855	0.847	0.840	0.833
2	1.713	1.690	1.668	1.647	1.626	1.605	1.585	1.566	1.547	1.528
3	2.444	2.402	2.361	2.322	2.283	2.246	2.210	2.174	2.140	2.106
4	3.102	3.037	2.974	2.914	2.855	2.798	2.743	2.690	2.639	2.589
5	3.696	3.605	3.517	3.433	3.352	3.274	3.199	3.127	3.058	2.991
6	4.231	4.111	3.998	3.889	3.784	3.685	3.589	3.498	3.410	3.326
7	4.712	4.564	4.423	4.288	4.160	4.039	3.922	3.812	3.706	3.605
8	5.146	4.968	4.799	4.639	4.487	4.344	4.207	4.078	3.954	3.837
9	5.537	5.328	5.132	4.946	4.772	4.607	4.451	4.303	4.163	4.031
10	5.889	5.650	5.426	5.216	5.019	4.833	4.659	4.494	4.339	4.192
11	6.207	5.938	5.687	5.453	5.234	5.029	4.836	4.656	4.486	4.327
12	6.492	6.194	5.918	5.660	5.421	5.197	4.988	4.793	4.611	4.439
13	6.750	6.424	6.122	5.842	5.583	5.342	5.118	4.910	4.715	4.533
14	6.982	6.628	6.302	6.002	5.724	5.468	5.229	5.008	4.802	4.611
15	7.191	6.811	6.462	6.142	5.847	5.575	5.324	5.092	4.876	4.675
16	7.379	6.974	6.604	6.265	5.954	5.668	5.405	5.162	4.938	4.730
17	7.549	7.120	6.729	6.373	6.047	5.749	5.475	5.222	4.990	4.775
18	7.702	7.250	6.840	6.467	6.128	5.818	5.534	5.273	5.033	4.812
19	7.839	7.366	6.938	6.550	6.198	5.877	5.584	5.316	5.070	4.843
20	7.963	7.469	7.025	6.623	6.259	5.929	5.628	5.353	5.101	4.870

APPENDIX E
FREQUENTLY USED SYMBOLS

A/P	Accounts payable	g	Growth rate; g_t is the growth rate in Period t
A/R	Account receivable		
β	Beta coefficient	HPR	Holding period return
b	Retention ratio	I%	Interest rate, rate of return, or YTM
BP	Break point		
CAPM	Capital Asset Pricing Model	IRR	Internal rate of return
		m	Compounding frequency
CF	Cash flow; CF_t is the cash flow in Period t	μ	Mean or average
		NOPAT	Net operating profit after taxes
D	(1) Dividend per share; D_t is the dividend in Period t	NPV	Net present value
	(2) Total market value of debt	NWC	Net working capital
		P	(1) Price of share of stock; P_0 = price of stock today
Δ	Difference or change		
DCF	Discounted cash flow		
DGM	Dividend growth model		(2) Price per unit of output
E	Market value of equity		
EAT	Earnings after taxes		(3) Market value of preferred stock
EBIT	Earnings before interest and Taxes		
		PBP	Payback period
EBT	Earnings before taxes	P/E	Price/earnings ratio
EFN	External Funds Needed	PI	Profitability index
EPS	Earnings per share	PMT	(1) Annuity payment
F	Fixed operating costs		(2) Calculator keystroke indicating payment
FCF	Free cash flow		
FV	Future value; FV_n is the future value in Period n	PV	Present value
		PV_A	Present value of an annuity
FYE	Fiscal year end		
		PV_{AD}	Present value of an

	annuity due		(2) Time
Q	Unit sales	TIE	Times interest earned
R_D	Cost of debt	TVM	Time value of money
R_E	Cost of equity	V	(1) Value
R_f	Risk free rate		(2) Variable cost per unit
R_M	Return on the market		(3) Total market value
R_{NE}	Cost of new equity	w	Weight or proportion
R_P	Cost of preferred stock	w_D	Weight of debt
R_{RE}	Cost of retained earnings	w_P	Weight of preferred stock
ROA	Return on assets	w_E	Weight of common equity
ROE	Return on equity		
RP	Risk premium	WACC	Weighted average cost of Capital
S	Dollar sales		
Σ	Summation sign	WMCC	Weighted marginal cost of capital
σ	Standard deviation		
T	(1) Tax rate	YTC	Yield to call
		YTM	Yield to maturity

APPENDIX F
SOLUTIONS TO END-OF-CHAPTER PROBLEMS

Chapter 1
1. E. Maximize shareholder value
2. C. Limited liability company
3. B. Capital budgeting
4. E. All of the above
5. C. Capital structure
6. C. Sole proprietorship
7. D. Easy and inexpensive to form
8. D. Financial management
9. B. Corporation
10. C. Maximizing current value per share

Chapter 2
1. A. Average tax rate
2. B. $162,500
3. E. 35%
4. C. $5.20
5. A. $22,250
6. B. increases; increasing
7. A. Marginal tax rate
8. C. Balance sheet
9. A. Inventory
10. A. Real assets

Chapter 3
1. E. Restating each item on the balance sheet as a percentage of total liabil ties and owners equity
2. A. 2.5%

3. B. 20%
4. B. $629
5. A. $15
6. C. Fixed assets
7. B. More
8. C. 0.70
9. B. 16.50%
10. A. 31.52%

Chapter 4
1. E. None of the above
2. D. Held constant
3. B. Judgmental Approach
4. C. Cash Budget
5. C. $88
6. D. $165
7. C. $55
8. C. $1,110
9. D. $565
10. C. Long-term debt

Chapter 5
1. B. 7.43%
2. C. $66,389.24
3. C. 14.86%
4. D. $16,502
5. C. 9 years
6. A. Compounding
7. A. $(1 + I\%)^N$
8. B. $620.84
9. B. Take the $3,500,000 because it has a higher present value

Financial Management: A Practical Guide to Value Creation   297

  10. B. $69.60

Chapter 6
1. E. 9.06%
2. E. 2.96 years
3. A. $830.36
4. D. $29,892.88
5. D. $2,603.90
6. B. Sell at a premium
7. C. $924.18
8. C. 12%
9. A. $32.35
10. A. $33.49

Chapter 7
1. C. $3,380.78
2. D. If the project has a profitability index greater than one the project should be accepted.
3. C. 2.0 years
4. D. $480.00
5. A. 23 percent
6. D Profitability index
7. C. $34,737
8. E. 16.3%; no
9. D. 4 years
10. C. 1.04; yes

Chapter 8
1. D. Incremental cash flows
2. A. Sunk cost
3. D. Forecasting risk
4. D. Operating cash flow
5. D. Interest

6. D. Additions to retained earnings
7. C. $81,250
8. D. $406,250
9. D. $431,250
10. D. -$48,163.16

Chapter 9
1. B. 8.59%
2. C. 12%
3. D. 19.29%
4. C. 9.9%
5. A. 11.28%
6. D. Capital structure weights
7. C. Weighted average cost of capital (WACC)
8. D. Is the return that the firm's creditors demand for new borrowings
9. B. Will decrease the WACC of a firm with some debt in its capital structure
10. D 10.5%

Chapter 10
1. A. Systematic plus non-systematic risk
2. E. In general, the higher the expected return the higher the risk
3. B. U.S. Treasury bills
4. C. 8.00%
5. C. 3.16%
6. D. Normal
7. B. The income component
8. D. 19.4%
9. A. $0
10. C. 0.0%

GLOSSARY

Accrual Basis Accounting – Revenue is recognized when earned and expenses when incurred.

Amortization Table – Instrument is used to illustrate the payment of debt over time. The table is comprised of five columns: (1) beginning balance, (2) payment amount, (3) interest portion, (4) principal portion, and (5) ending balance.

Annuity Due – Cash flows that occur at the beginning of each period for some fixed number of periods.

Average Tax Rate - The percentage of income used to pay taxes. It is calculated by dividing total taxes paid by total taxable income.

Arithmetic Return – The simple average return, which is calculated as the sum of the individual holding period returns divided by the number of returns.

Balance Sheet – A financial statement that takes a still photograph of the firm on a particular day. The balance sheet includes assets, liabilities, and shareholders' equity.

Beta – A measure of riskiness of an equity security in comparison to the broad market.

Bond – A debt security that is an interest-only loan, meaning that the borrower will pay the interest every period, but none of the principal will be repaid until maturity. With a bond, the coupon is the stated interest payments made on the loan and the face value is the principal amount of the bond that will be repaid at maturity.

Bond Ratings – An assessment of the creditworthiness of the corporate issuer. At present, there are two leading bond-rating firms: Moody's and Standard and Poor's.

Business Model – A company's strategy that includes: (1) the nature of the business, (2) the industry and sector in which it operates, (3) the company's organizational structure, (4) its primary competitors, and (5) the company's sources of competitive advantage.

Capital Budgeting – The process of planning and managing a firm's long-term investments opportunities. In capital budgeting, the financial manager tries to identify investment opportunities where the value of the cash flow generated by the project exceeds the cost of the investment.

Capital Rationing – The process of allocating budgeted funds among competing capital expenditures.

Capital Spending – Refers to the net spending on fixed assets (purchase of fixed assets less sales of fixed assets).

Capital Structure – A firm's capital structure refers to the specific mixture of debt (commercial loans and fixed income securities) and equity (retained earnings, common stock, and preferred stock) the firm uses to finance its operations and investment opportunities.

Cash Basis Accounting - Recognizes revenue when received and expenses when paid.

Cash Budget – A statement of the company's planned inflows and outflows of cash over a fixed period of time.

Cash Disbursements – All of the company's cash outflow for a given period, including wages, rent, principal and interest payments, dividend payments, and tax payments

Cash Flow – The measure of the flow of funds (i.e., cash) into and out of the company over a historical period of time.

Cash Receipts – All of the company's cash inflows for a given period, which are divided into three categories: cash sales, accounts receivable, and other.

Change in Net Working Capital – The amount spent on net working capital. It is measured as the change in current assets and current liabilities over the period being examined.

Common-Size Statements – The process to standardize the financial statements in which dollars must be converted to percentages. To create a common size balance sheet, each item on the balance sheet must be expressed as a percentage of total assets or total liabilities and owner's equity. Similarly, to standardize the income statement, we need to express each item as a percentage of total sales.

Compound Interest – Interest earned on original principal and prior year's interest.

Compounding Period - The period of time required to meet your investment goals. This period can range from weekly to quarterly to annually.

Conventional Cash Flow Patterns – An investment opportunity that requires an initial cash outflow that is followed by a series of cash inflows.

Corporation – A legal "person" separate and distinct from the owners. As such, corporations can borrow money and own property, can sue and be sued, and can enter into contractual arrangements.

Cost of Debt – The return that the firm's creditors demand on new borrowing. The interest rate the firm must pay on new borrowing.

Cost of Equity Capital – The return that equity investors require on their investment in the firm. There are two approaches to determining the cost of equity: dividend growth model (DGM) approach and the capital asset pricing model (CAPM) approach.

Cost of Preferred Stock – It is simply equal to the dividend yield on preferred stock.

Coupon Rate – The annual coupon payment expressed as a percentage of the face value of the bond.

Current Assets - Those assets that can be turned into cash relatively quickly. Cash, accounts receivable, and inventory are examples of current assets.

Current Liabilities – The debt that the company is obligated to pay back within one year. Accounts payable is a good example.

Current Yield – The annual coupon payment expressed as a percentage of the current price of the bond.

Decision Tree – A diagram made up of nodes and branches. The nodes denote decision points and the branches represent alternative decisions and their associated probability.

Depreciation – Represents an adjustment for the use of the asset each year. Also appears on the income statement as a non-cash expense.

Discount Rate – Also known as the rate of return, denoted as I% is the return on the investment. It is used to compare the performance of two or more investments over time.

Earnings Per Share – Used to express profits or losses on a per share basis. It is calculated by dividing net income (or loss) by shares outstanding.

Erosion – Cost that occurs when the cash flows of a new project come at the expense of a company's existing projects.

External Funds Needed – The amount of external financing (i.e., debt and equity capital) that would be needed to reach a particular growth rate in the next period.

Financial Planning – The process of forecasting a company's future growth.

Free Cash Flow (FCF) – The cash flow actually available for distribution to investors after the company has made all the investments in fixed assets and working capital necessary to sustain ongoing operations.

Forecasting Risk – The possibility that management will make a bad investment decisions because of errors in the projected cash flows associated with the investment proposal.

Future Value - Refers to the cash value of an investment at some point in the future.

General Partnership – A business venture in which two or more partners engage. All the partners share in gains or losses, and all have unlimited liability for all partnership debts.

Geometric Return – The compound average return.

Income Statement – The income statement measures the performance of a business over some period of time, usually on a quarterly or annual basis. A basic income statement is constructed by subtracting various expenses from revenue.

Independent Projects – Those projects that are not related to one another; in other words, accepting one project does not eliminate the acceptance of another.

Initial Investment – The relevant cash outflows

associated with a proposed capital expenditure that occur at T_0.

Internal Growth Rate – The growth rate a company can achieve without having to raise additional funds (i.e., debt and equity) through the capital markets.

Internal Rate of Return (IRR) – The discount rate that sets the net present value of an investment equal to zero. In other words, it is a single rate of return that summarizes the merits of a project. If the projects' IRR exceeds the required return, it is a viable investment; it should be rejected otherwise.

Investment Grade – The term used to describe bonds rated BBB (S&P) or Baa (Moody's) or better. Any debt rated below a BBB is considered non-investment grade or "junk."

Limited Liability Company (LLC) – A relatively new type of business entity, and is one of the most versatile. An LLC is created under state law by filing articles of organization, which are similar to articles of incorporation filed by a corporation. . An LLC provides the limited personal liability of a corporation and the flow-through taxation of partnerships and S corporations.

Limited Partnership – A business venture in which two or more partners engage. There are one or more limited partners who do not actively participate in the business. A limited partner's liability for business debts is limited to the amount that he or she (s/he) contributes.

Long-term Assets – Also known, as fixed assets are usable for more than one year, include property, plant, and equipment. Fixed assets can either be tangible, such as office equipment or an automobile, or intangible, such as a trademark, copyright, or patent.

Long-term Liability – Debt that is not due in the next 12 months is classified as a long-term liability.

Marginal Tax Rate – The amount of tax payable on the next dollar of income earned.

Mutually Exclusive Projects – Projects that compete with one another; in other words, the acceptance of one eliminates considerations of all other similar projects.

Net Present Value (NPV) – The difference between an investment's discounted cash flows (i.e., market value) and its initial cost. A project with a NPV > 0 should be accepted.

Operating Cash Flow – Cash flow generated by the company's day-to-day activities. Funds associated with the company's financing activities are not included since they are not operating expenses.

Opportunity Costs – Costs that typically arise when the firm owns some of the assets needed for the proposed project. Thus, opportunity cost is the most valuable alternative that is given up if a particular investment is undertaken.

Ordinary Annuity – Cash flows that occur at the end of each period for some fixed number of periods.

Payback Period – The length of time it takes to recover the initial investment of a project. Due to the simplicity of the calculation, payback period is a useful tool in evaluating small projects.

Peer Group Analysis – Analyze a company's financial ratios by comparing them to firms that are similar in the sense that they compete in the same markets, have similar assets or operate in similar ways.

Percentage of Sales Approach - Most common method used in determining external funds needed. The process has two main steps: create pro forma income statements and balance sheets for the next period, and using the projected balance sheet, calculate the difference between total assets and total liabilities and owner's equity.

Pro Forma Financial Statements – Statements that are used to illustrate a proposed change or future projections. They provide a convenient and easily understood means of summarizing relevant information for a project.

Preferred Stock – It is considered a hybrid security; it has a fixed dividend paid each period forever, so it is considered a perpetuity.

Present Value – Represents the amount that must be invested today to reach a particular investment goal.

Profitability Index – The present value of the future cash flows divided by the cost of the investment. A project, with a profitability index greater than 1.00, indicates that the project adds value to the owners of the company.

Relevant Cash Flows – Any and all changes to a company's future cash flows that are a direct consequence of adopting a project.

Rule of 72 - Whenever you are presented with a problem that involves doubling your money this method can be used. The Rule of 72 states that the number of periods needed to double your money is equal to 72 / I%.

S Corporation – A special type of corporation for federal income tax purposes. The corporation is formed in a manner similar to that of a regular corporation; however, it is treated similar to a partnership for income tax purposes.

Salvage Value – A price that any fixed assets will be able to be sold for at the end of a project's life.

Scenario Analysis – The changes in earnings and NPV estimates that result from asking questions like "What if unit sales realistically should be projected at 20,000 units instead of 24,000 units?"

Sensitivity Analysis – Freezing all of the variables on a pro forma statement except one in order to determine the sensitivity of estimate to change sin that one variable.

Shareholder Equity - The difference between the value of the company's assets and the value of liabilities (or debt) outstanding is referred to as shareholder' equity. Equity is typically comprised of common and preferred stock, paid in capital, and retained earnings.

Simple Interest – Interest earned on original principal only.

Simulation – An analytical tool used to evaluate the effect of varying inputs (assumption cells) on the model output (forecast cell).

Sole Proprietorship – A business owned by one person. This is the simplest, least regulated, and most common form of organization. The owner keeps all the profits but have unlimited liability for business debts.

Source of Cash - Activities that bring cash into the company.

Standard Deviation - a statistical measure of the variability around the expected or mean return. The higher the variability, the higher the risk.

Sunk Costs – Costs that have already been paid or costs that the company has incurred the liability to pay. These costs cannot be changed by our decision to accept or reject the project.

Sustainable Growth Rate - The attainable growth rate if the company maintains its current debt ratio and does not issue any new equity.

Systematic Risk - The risk of the "system" or market. It includes changes in interest rates, inflation rates, and other world events that affect all securities. It cannot be diversified away.

Terminal Cash Flow – The after-tax nonoperating cash flow occurring in the final year of a project. It is the cash flow attributable to the salvage value of the equipment and other assets used for the project, net of any removal and cleanup costs.

Time Trend Analysis – Analyzing the financial ratios of a single company over several periods of time.

Time Value of Money – Refers to the fact that a dollar in hand today is worth more than a dollar promised at some point in the future.

Unsystematic Risk – risk specific to the company or industry in which the company operates. It can be diversified away through a portfolio of 18–40 securities.

Use of Cash – Activities that involve spending cash and remove cash from the firm.

Weighted Average Cost of Capital (WACC) – This is the firm's overall cost of capital. The capital structure weights are multiplied by the associated costs. The sum of the different weighted costs generates WACC.

Working Capital – Refers to a firm's short-term assets, such as cash, accounts receivable, and inventory, and its short-term liabilities, such as money owned to the government and business partners.

INDEX

A

Accrual Basis Accounting	52
Additions To Retained Earnings	51
Amortization	153
Annualized Return	256
Annualized Standard Deviation	258
Annuities	149
Annuity Compounding Period	152
Annuity Interest Rate	153
Annuity Payment	151
Arithmetic Return	246, 247, 256
Assets	55, 81
Average Tax Rate	54

B

Balance Sheet	54
Benchmark	30, 81
Beta	248, 250, 258
Bond Ratings	224
Book Value	55

C

Capital Sources	71
Capital Spending	69
Capital Budgeting	28
Capital Rationing	176
Capital Structure	28
Cash Basis Accounting	51
Cash Budget	100
Cash Coverage Ratio	83
Cash Flow	58, 68
From Assets	68
Common Size Statements	75
Compound Interest	134
Compounding Period	138
Corporations	33
Cost Of Debt Capital	221
Cost Of Equity Capital	226
Cost Of Preferred Stock	230
Coupon Rate	222
Crystal Ball	112
Current Liabilities	71
Current Ratio	55, 79
Current Yield	222

D

Days' Sales In Inventory	83
Days' Sales In Receivables	84
Debt-To-Equity Ratio	82
Decision Trees	201
Depreciation Conventions	188
Discount Rate	137, 138
Distribution	
Normal	117
Triangular	117
Uniform	117
Dividend Growth Model	226
Dividend Payout Ratio	87, 104
Dividends	51, 186

E

Earnings Per Share	50
Efficiency Ratios	83
Emperical Rule	249
External Funds Needed	108

F

Financial Assets	54
Financial Leverage	54
Financial Management	27
Financial Strength Ratios	79
Forecasting Risk	198
Forecasting Units Sold	112
Free Cash Flow	71
Future Value (FV)	132
Of An Annuity	150
Of Multiple Cash Flows	145

G

Geometric Average	247
Geometric Return	247
Gross Investment In Operating Capital	74
Gross Margin	84

H

Holding Period Return 245, 249

I

Income Statement	48
Initial Investment	187
Intangible Assets	55
Interest Coverage Ratio	82
Interest Expense	186
Interest Rates And Bond Values	224
Internal Growth Rate	104
Internal Rate Of Return	173
Inventory	81
Inventory Turnover	83

L

Latin Hypercube Sampling Method	119
Liabilities & Owner's Equity	56
Limited Liability Company	36
Liquid Assets	55
Long-term Assets	55

M

MACRS	189
Management Effectiveness Ratios	86
Marginal Tax Rate	53
Measures Of Return	244
Monte Carlo Sampling Method	119
Multexnet	
Company Analysis	43
Identifying Competitors	76
Income Statement	48
Industry Analysis	45

N

Net Investment In Operating Capital	73
Net Present Value	171, 198
Net Profit Margin	85

Net Working Capital	70	Return On Equity (ROE)	86
NOPAT	73, 75	Return On Equity Securities: Capital Asset Pricing Model Approach	228

O

Operating Cash Flow	69, 192	Risk	243
		Measures of Risk	248
Operating Profit Margin	85		
Opportunity Cost	186		

S

S Corporation	36
Sales Forecast	112

P

Partnerships	32	Salvage Value	189
Payback Period	175	Scenario Analysis	198
Payout Ratios	87	Sensitivity Analysis	199
Peer Group Analysis	87	Sharpe Ratio	259
Present Value (PV)	135	SIC Codes	75
Of An Annuity	149	Simple Interest	133
Of Multiple Cash Flows	148	Simulation	116, 203
Pro Forma Financial Statements	112, 113, 200	Sole Proprietorship	32
		Sources And Uses Of Cash	66
Profitability Index	176	Standard Deviation	248, 257
Profitability Ratios	84	Sunk Costs	186
Project Cash Flows	186	Sustainable Growth Rate	105

Q

T

Quick Ratio	81	Taxes	52
		Terminal Cash Flow	194

R

		Total Asset Turnover	84
Ratio Analysis	79	Total Debt Ratio	82
Real Assets	54		

V

Receivables Turnover	84		
Retention Ratio	87	Valuing Debt Securities	156
Return	243	Valuing Equity Securities	160
Return On Assets (ROA)	86		
Return On Debt Securities	222		

W

Weighted Average Cost Of Capital 231

Y

Yield To Maturity 222